# DAS MINIMUM ENGLISCH TRAINING

**Ute Herwig / Christina Mecke**

# DAS MINIMUM ENGLISCH TRAINING

# Inhalt

| | | |
|---|---|---|
| **Vorwort** | | 5 |
| **Dialoge** | 1 Hotel | 7 |
| | 2 Frühstück im Hotel | 12 |
| | 3 Telefonieren mit Geld (USA) | 16 |
| | 4 Telefonieren ohne Geld (USA) | 21 |
| | 5 Arzt | 24 |
| | 6 Apotheke | 28 |
| | 7 Post | 32 |
| | 8 Supermarkt | 35 |
| | 9 Andenkenladen | 38 |
| | 10 Restaurant | 42 |
| | 11 Nachtleben | 45 |
| | 12 Pub | 48 |
| | 13 Getränke bestellen | 53 |
| | 14 Wetter | 56 |
| | 15 nach dem Weg fragen | 60 |
| | 16 Auto | 64 |
| | 17 Fremdenverkehrsbüro | 68 |
| | 18 Bahnhof | 73 |
| **Korrespondenz** | 19 Hotelreservierung | 76 |
| | 20 Einen Flug buchen | 81 |
| | 21 Privates | 85 |
| | 22 Liebe | 88 |
| | 23 Geburtstag | 91 |
| | 24 Weihnachten | 94 |
| | 25 Große Feste | 97 |
| | 26 Kleine Feiern | 99 |
| | 27 Unvorhersehbare Umstände | 102 |
| | 28 Vielen Dank | 105 |
| | 29 Ferien | 108 |
| **Lösungen** | | 113 |

# Vorwort

Liebe Leserin, lieber Leser,

möglicherweise planen Sie gerade eine Reise nach England oder in die USA, haben aber Bedenken, ob Ihre Englischkenntnisse ausreichen, um kleine Alltagssituationen problemlos zu meistern.
Womöglich wollen Sie auch nicht nach England, haben aber trotzdem den Wunsch, Ihre Englischkenntnisse aus der Schulzeit wieder aufzufrischen.
Vielleicht besuchen Sie bereits einen Englischkursus für Englisch und wollen in Eigeninitiative Ihre Sprachkenntnisse erweitern.
Oder Sie sind der langweiligen Englischlehrwerke überdrüssig und suchen ein kleines Buch, das auf amüsante und leicht verständliche Art ein authentisches Englisch präsentiert und gleichzeitig für jede Gelegenheit die passenden **Wendungen und Begriffe** bereithält.

Dann haben Sie gerade das Gesuchte in der Hand. Dieses handliche Lehrwerk bietet pointierte Alltagsdialoge in englischer Sprache für diverse Situationen an den verschiedensten Orten.
Gebräuchliche Redensarten, Meinungsäußerungen und das ein oder andere passende Schimpfwort machen die Dialoge lebendig und lebensnah. Durch überraschende Wendungen, Missverständnisse und Situationskomik innerhalb der Dialoge wird die Lektüre dieses kleinen Buches nicht nur zu einem vergnüglichen Zeitvertreib, sondern auch zu einem lehrreichen Kursus.

Zusätzlich zu den Alltagsdialogen finden Sie diverse nützliche Vorschläge zur schriftlichen Korrespondenz. Die Hotelreservierung im Ausland oder die Feriengrüße an englischsprachige Freunde werden Ihnen mit dieser Hilfe leicht von der Hand gehen. Die einzelnen Einheiten sind sehr kurz und beanspruchen daher wenig Zeitaufwand. Als ständiger Begleiter kann dieses Büchlein beispielsweise lästige Wartezeiten sinnvoll ausfüllen oder als Soforthilfe vor Ort dienen – falls Sie doch nach England reisen wollen.

Als Verständnishilfen dienen für jeden Text die deutsche Übersetzung und die Vokabelangaben. Außerdem können Sie Ihr erlangtes Wissen anhand kurzweiliger Übungen überprüfen. Diese finden Sie jeweils am Ende der deutschen Übersetzung.
Der Lösungsteil für die Übungsaufgaben befindet sich im dritten Abschnitt des Buches ab Seite 113.

Viel Spaß beim Lernen, Lesen und Lachen!

# Dialoge

## 1 Hotel

**Tell that to the marines!**

A woman enters the hotel lobby and walks over to the reception desk.

| | |
|---|---|
| receptionist: | Good morning, Madam. Can I help you? |
| woman: | I hope so. My room number is 208. I booked a <u>half board single-room</u> with a shower, a TV set and a telephone. |
| receptionist: | That's right. What's the problem? |
| woman: | Where's the television, for example? |
| receptionist: | It's in your room. |
| woman: | No it is not. |
| receptionist: | Ah! Then I'll ask the room maid where the TV set could be. She knows where the TV's usually hang around . |
| woman: | TV's don't hang around. They're normally just there and don't move. |
| receptionist: | Some do and some don't. |
| woman: | Will you please be so kind and persuade one of the TV's to hang around in my room? |
| receptionist: | Yes, certainly. I'll try my best. |
| woman: | Thank you very much. |
| receptionist: | Leave it all to me. It is my job to make your stay in our house a real holiday. |
| woman: | There is another little problem. Last night I saw a little mouse in the <u>shower cabin.</u> |
| receptionist: | That can't be. We have no mice in our hotel. Maybe you saw our hotel ghost. |

| | |
|---|---|
| woman: | I can distinguish between a mouse and a hotel ghost. I tell you, it was a mouse. |
| receptionist: | Just one question. What did it look like? Was it small, hairy, brown, with four legs and did it look like a mouse? |
| woman: | Yes, it did. |
| receptionist: | Then I can assure you that you saw our hotel ghost. |
| woman: | If your little ghost crosses my path a second time, <u>I will put its immortality to the test.</u> |

| | |
|---:|---|
| to book | buchen |
| room maid | Zimmermädchen |
| to hang around | herum hängen |
| to persuade | überreden |
| to distinguish | unterscheiden |
| ghost | Gespenst |
| hairy | pelzig |
| to assure | versichern |
| immortality | Unsterblichkeit |

*Dialoge*

## Das können Sie Ihrer Großmutter erzählen!

Eine Frau betritt die Eingangshalle eines Hotels und geht zur Rezeption.

Rezeption: Guten Morgen. Kann ich Ihnen helfen?
Frau: Das hoffe ich doch. Ich habe die Zimmernummer 208. Ich habe ein Einzelzimmer mit Halbpension gebucht, mit einer Dusche, einem Fernseher und einem Telefon.
Rezeption: Richtig. Wo ist das Problem?
Frau: Wo ist zum Beispiel der Fernseher?
Rezeption: Er ist in Ihrem Zimmer.
Frau: Nein, ist er nicht.
Rezeption: Dann werde ich das Zimmermädchen fragen, wo der Fernseher sein könnte. Sie wird wissen, wo die Fernseher normalerweise rumhängen.
Frau: Fernseher hängen nicht herum. Sie sind normalerweise einfach da und bewegen sich nicht.
Rezeption: Einige machen das und andere nicht.
Frau: Würden Sie dann so freundlich sein und eines der Fernsehgeräte dazu überreden, in meinem Zimmer rumzuhängen?
Rezeption: Ja, natürlich. Ich werde mein Bestes versuchen.
Frau: Haben Sie vielen Dank.
Rezeption: Überlassen Sie das ruhig mir. Es ist meine Aufgabe, aus Ihrem Aufenthalt in unserem Haus einen gelungenen Urlaub zu machen.
Frau: Da gibt es noch ein kleines Problem. Letzten Abend habe ich eine kleine Maus in meiner Duschkabine gesehen.
Rezeption: Das kann nicht sein. Wir haben keine Mäuse in

| | |
|---|---|
| | unserem Hotel. Vielleicht haben Sie unseren Hotelgeist gesehen. |
| Frau: | Ich bin in der Lage, zwischen einem Hotelgeist und einer Maus zu unterscheiden. Ich sage Ihnen, es war eine Maus. |
| Rezeption: | Nur eine Frage. Wie sah es aus? War es klein, behaart, braun und hatte es vier Beine und sah aus wie eine Maus? |
| Frau: | Ja, das tat es. |
| Rezeption: | Dann kann ich Ihnen versichern, dass Sie unseren Hotelgeist gesehen haben. |
| Frau: | Wenn Ihr kleiner Geist ein zweites Mal meinen Weg kreuzt, werde ich nachprüfen, ob er unsterblich ist. |

## Übersetzen Sie bitte die Sätze ins Englische.

1. Ich habe Zimmernummer 208.

   _____

2. Es gibt ein Problem mit der Dusche.

   _____

3. Können Sie mir helfen?

   _____

4. Ich werde mein Bestes versuchen.

   _____

5. Wo ist das Telefon?

___

6. Wo ist die Rezeption?

___

7. Würden Sie so nett sein?

___

8. Da ist noch ein kleines Problem.

___

9. Überlassen Sie das ruhig mir.

___

10. Ich sage Ihnen, ich habe eine Maus gesehen!

___

## 2  Frühstück im Hotel

**The spirit is willing, but the flesh is weak**

A couple is sitting in the restaurant of a hotel.

waiter: Good morning. What would you like as a starter?
woman: I'd like some corn flakes with milk and honey.
man: Don't do it, darling. Any food scientist would warn you. Honey and sugar are poison to your body. I'll just have an orange juice, please.

The waiter brings the ordered things and comes back after ten minutes.

waiter: And what would you like for the main course?
woman: I'd like scrambled eggs, sausages and baked beans. Oh, and a cup of coffee, please.
man: That'll kill you. It's too greasy. One should not eat such things in the morning. Waiter, just give me a small portion of porridge, please, and a cup of tea.
woman: Steve! Live and let live, will you?

Fifteen minutes later, the waiter comes back.

waiter: Would you like something else?
woman: I think that will do. Just another cup of coffee, please.
man: Remember the risks of drinking too much coffee, darling.
woman: Yes, I will remember later.
man: Hm, I'm still a little hungry. One shouldn't start the day without having had a good breakfast. I think I'll have ham and eggs, sausages, fried tomatoes and baked beans and kipper, please.

*Dialoge*

| | |
|---:|:---|
| food scientist | **Ernährungswissenschaftler/in** |
| poison | **Gift** |
| main course | **Hauptgericht** |
| scrambled eggs | **Rühreier** |
| sausages | **Bratwürstchen** |
| baked beans | **gebackene Bohnen** |
| greasy | **fettig** |
| porridge | **Haferbrei** |
| to live and let live | **leben und leben lassen** |
| risk | **Gefahr** |
| ham and eggs | **Schinken und Eier (gebraten)** |
| fried tomatoes | **frittierte Tomaten** |
| kipper | **Räucherfisch** |

## Der Geist ist willig, aber das Fleisch ist schwach

Ein Paar sitzt im Restaurant eines Hotels.

| | |
|:---|:---|
| Bedienung: | Guten Morgen. Was möchten Sie als ersten Gang? |
| Frau: | Ich hätte gerne Cornflakes mit Milch und Honig. |
| Mann: | Tu das nicht, Liebling. Jeder Ernährungswissenschaftler wird dich warnen. Honig und Zucker sind Gift für deinen Körper. Ich hätte gerne nur einen Orangensaft. |

Die Bedienung bringt die bestellten Sachen und kommt nach zehn Minuten wieder.

| | |
|:---|:---|
| Bedienung: | Und was hätten Sie gern als Hauptgang? |
| Frau: | Ich hätte gerne Rühreier, Bratwürstchen und gebackene Bohnen. Oh, und eine Tasse Kaffee, bitte. |
| Mann: | Das wird dich umbringen, wenn du damit nicht aufhörst, Liebling. Es ist zu fettig. Man |

|            | sollte solche Sachen nicht morgens essen. Bedienung, bringen Sie mir bitte nur eine kleine Portion Haferbrei und eine Tasse Tee. |
|------------|---|
| Frau:      | Steve! Leben und leben lassen, kannst du das? |

Die Bedienung kommt fünfzehn Minuten später zurück.

| Bedienung: | Wünschen Sie noch etwas? |
|------------|---|
| Frau:      | Ich glaube das reicht. Nur noch eine Tasse Kaffee, bitte. |
| Mann:      | Erinnere dich bitte an die Risiken durch zu viel Kaffeegenuss. |
| Frau:      | Ja, ich werde mich nachher daran erinnern. |
| Mann:      | Hm, ich habe immer noch ein bisschen Hunger. Man sollte den Tag nicht ohne ein gutes Frühstück beginnen. Ich glaube, ich brauche noch Schinken und Eier, Bratwürstchen, gegrillte Tomaten, gebackene Bohnen und Räucherfisch, bitte. |

**Englisches Frühstück**

Das Frühstück in Großbritannien ist nicht jedermanns Sache. Die meisten Briten bevorzugen ein üppiges und warmes Gericht, das sich sehr von kontinentalen Speisen unterscheidet. Wer morgens schon gebratene kleine Würstchen oder Bückling verträgt und auch nichts gegen gebackene Kidneybohnen in Tomatensoße hat, der ist in Großbritannien richtig aufgehoben. Brötchen wird man suchen müssen.
Dafür gibt es Toast und Orangenmarmelade. Da Briten Teetrinker sind, darf man vom Kaffee nicht viel erwarten. Er ist in der Regel dünn und geschmacksarm.
Inzwischen wird in den meisten Hotels ein internationales Frühstück serviert.

## A  Ein Kreuzworträtsel

Setzen Sie bitte die unten angegebenen Wörter ein!

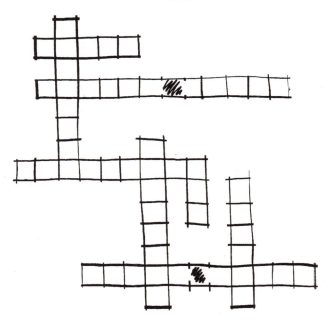

**tea**
**sausages**
**breakfast**
**orange juice**

**coffee**
**baked beans**
**porridge**
**toast**

## B  Ein Rätsel

What starts with "T", ends with "T" and is full of "T"?

## 3   Telefonieren mit Geld (USA)

**That sounds easy!**

A man walks along a street in a city and stops a woman coming along.

man: Excuse me, Madam. Would you be so kind as to tell me how to use a telephone box?

woman: Yes, I will. Listen! From a phone booth in the USA there are two ways to call out. The first way is to use coins, but then you must have enough coins ready. If it is a long distance call out of the state you are in, you must dial a 1 first. Then you dial the area code. Every state has an area code and some very big states have more than one area code.

man: What would be the area code for Indiana for example?

woman: It is 317.

man: Okay, and then I put the coins in?

woman: No, you dial 1 plus the area code and the rest of your number and then a nice computer voice will tell you how many coins you have to put in the machine.

man: What about using a credit card?

woman: That would be the second way to telephone. If you use a credit card instead of coins, you have to dial a 0 instead of 1. Therefore it would be 0 - 317 - and the rest of your number. Then a voice will come on the phone and tell you which phone company it is and to enter your private code. Your private code is usually your home phone number

|  | plus a 4 digit PIN code. For example 0-317-545-1234-3424. In this case 3424 would be your PIN code. The computer voice then thanks you for using their company and you are connected. |
|---|---|
| man: | That sounds easy. I will try it out with this booth right here. I think I have enough coins. Where is the receiver? I can't find the receiver! This booth is out of order! |
| woman: | No, it isn't; what you have here is not a booth but a coke machine. |

| | |
|---:|:---|
| booth | Telefonzelle |
| coins | Münzen |
| long distance call | Ferngespräch |
| to dial | wählen |
| area code | Vorwahl |
| computer voice | Computerstimme |
| credit card | Kreditkarte |
| second way | zweite Möglichkeit |
| company | Gesellschaft |
| private code | Privatnummer |
| PIN (Personal Identification Number) | Geheimnummer |
| receiver | Hörer |
| coke machine | Getränkeautomat |

*Telefonieren mit Geld*

## Das klingt einfach!

Ein Mann geht in einer Stadt eine Straße entlang und hält eine vorbeikommende Frau an.

Mann: Entschuldigen Sie. Würden Sie so freundlich sein und mir erklären, wie man einen Münzfernsprecher benutzt?

Frau: Ja, das kann ich tun. Hören Sie zu. Es gibt in den USA zwei verschiedene Möglichkeiten, von einem Münzfernsprecher aus zu telefonieren. Bei der ersten Möglichkeit benutzen Sie Münzen, aber dann müssen Sie genügend davon parat haben. Wenn es sich um ein Ferngespräch außerhalb des Staates handelt, in dem Sie sich befinden, müssen Sie zunächst eine 1 wählen. Dann wählen Sie die Nummer des Staates. Jeder Staat hat eine Nummer und einige sehr große Staaten haben mehr als eine.

Mann: Was wäre beispielsweise die Nummer für Indiana?

Frau: Sie lautet 317.

Mann: Gut, und dann werfe ich die Münzen ein?

Frau: Nein. Sie wählen eine 1, die Nummer des Staates und den Rest Ihrer Nummer und dann wird eine nette Computerstimme Ihnen sagen, wie viele Münzen Sie einwerfen müssen.

Mann: Und wie sieht es aus, wenn ich eine Kreditkarte benutze?

Frau: Das wäre die zweite Möglichkeit zu telefonieren. Wenn Sie eine Kreditkarte anstelle von Münzen benutzen, müssen Sie eine 0 anstelle der 1 wählen. Dann wäre es die Nummer 0-317 und der Rest Ihrer Nummer. Dann wird eine Stimme zu hören sein, die Ihnen sagt, mit welcher Telefongesellschaft Sie verbunden sind, und dass Sie Ihre Privatnummer wählen sollen. Ihre Privatnummer ist gewöhnlich identisch mit Ihrer eigenen Telefonnummer und vier Geheimzahlen. Zum Beispiel 0-317-545-1234-3424. In diesem Fall wären die Zahlen 3424 Ihre Geheimzahlen. Die Computerstimme wird sich bei Ihnen dafür bedanken, dass Sie ihre Gesellschaft benutzt haben und dann werden Sie verbunden.

Mann: Das hört sich einfach an. Ich werde es mit diesem Münzfernsprecher hier versuchen. Ich glaube, ich habe genug Münzen. Wo ist der Hörer? Ich kann den Hörer nicht finden! Dieser Münzfernsprecher ist kaputt!

Frau: Nein, ist er nicht, aber was Sie hier haben ist gar kein Münzfernsprecher, sondern ein Getränkeautomat.

**A Schreiben Sie bitte eine Anleitung zum Telefonieren mit Münzen.
Bringen Sie dazu die nachstehenden Sätze in die korrekte Reihenfolge!**

1. A computer voice will tell you how many coins you have to put in.
2. Dial a 1 for long distance calls.
3. You are connected.
4. Have enough coins ready.
5. Dial the rest of the number.
6. Dial the area code.

**B Bringen Sie bitte auch die folgenden Sätze in die richtige Reihenfolge, damit eine korrekte Anleitung zum Telefonieren mit einer Kreditkarte für amerikanische Münzfernsprecher entsteht!**

1. You enter your home number plus a 4 digit PIN code.
2. Dial a 0 for long distance calls.
3. You are connected.
4. Dial the area code.
5. A computer voice thanks you.
6. A voice tells you to enter your private number.

**C Beantworten Sie bitte die folgenden Fragen:**

1. Aus welchen beiden Teilnummern besteht die *private number*?
2. Was ist ein *area code*?

## 4 Telefonieren ohne Geld (USA)

**Not a bean left!**

A woman and a man meet at a booth.

woman: Excuse me, Sir. I have to call my office but haven't got coins or a credit card. Would you mind telling me how calling collect works?

man: Yes, certainly. Dial a 0 and the number. It is the same number as when you have a credit card. A voice will ask you either to give your credit card number or to wait on the line for an operator. Then the computer voice will ask you to say your name after the "beep". Then you have to wait a little while the computer calls the number of the people you want to talk to. The computer will ask them "Will you accept a collect call from..." and then it will play back your name. If the people are at home and say "yes" you are connected. If not, you are disconnected.

woman: Have you got any experience in calling this way?

man: Yes, yesterday I wanted to ring up a friend of mine. We bet on horses and I wanted to know if we won.

woman: And did you win?

man: I don't think so. I knew that he was at home, but he didn't want to accept my call. Unfortunately, he didn't have enough money.

woman: Oh, bad luck!

| | |
|---|---|
| to play back | wiedergeben |
| experience | Erfahrung |
| to bet on horses | beim Pferderennen wetten |

# Kein Pfennig mehr übrig!

Eine Frau und ein Mann treffen sich an einer Telefonzelle.

Frau: Entschuldigen Sie. Ich muss in meinem Büro anrufen und habe weder Münzen noch eine Kreditkarte. Würden Sie so nett sein und mir erklären, wie ein R-Gespräch funktioniert?

Mann: Ja, natürlich. Wählen Sie eine 0 und die Nummer. Es ist dieselbe Nummer wie bei einer Kreditkarte. Eine Stimme wird sie auffordern, entweder eine Kreditkarte zu benutzen oder zu warten, bis die Vermittlung kommt. Dann wird die Vermittlung Sie auffordern, Ihren Namen nach dem "Piep"-Ton zu sagen. Dann müssen Sie ein bisschen warten, während die Vermittlung die Nummer der Leute wählt, die Sie sprechen möchten.
Der Computer wird die Leute fragen "Nehmen Sie ein R-Gespräch an?" Und dann wird er Ihren Namen, den Sie angegeben haben, wiedergeben. Wenn die Leute zu Hause sind und "ja" sagen, werden Sie verbunden. Wenn nicht, wird die Verbindung unterbrochen.

Frau: Haben Sie Erfahrungen mit dieser Art zu telefonieren?

Mann: Ja, gestern wollte ich einen Freund anrufen. Wir haben beim Pferderennen gewettet und ich wollte wissen, ob wir gewonnen haben.

Frau: Und, haben Sie gewonnen?

Mann: Ich glaube nicht. Ich wusste, dass er zu Hause ist, aber er hat den Anruf nicht angenommen. Unglücklicherweise hatte er nicht genügend Geld.

Frau: Oh, Sie Pechvogel!

## A Ordnen Sie bitte die Sätze so, dass eine Anleitung für ein R-Gespräch entsteht!

- [ ] A voice will tell you to wait for an operator.
- [ ] You say your name after the "beep".
- [ ] You are connected.
- [ ] The computer asks the people if they want to accept the call.
- [ ] Take the receiver.
- [ ] The voice asks you to say your name after the "beep."
- [ ] Dial an 0 and the rest of your number.
- [ ] The people say "yes".
- [ ] A computer calls the number of the people you want to talk to.

## B Übersetzen Sie bitte ins Englische!

1. Ich möchte ein R-Gespräch führen.
2. Ich hoffe, Sie werden den Anruf annehmen.
3. Ich warte auf die Vermittlung.
4. Die Leitung wurde unterbrochen.

# 5  Arzt

## A near miss

A woman enters a surgery.

woman: Good morning.
man: Good morning, Madam! Come in and take a seat, please.
woman: I've come, because I'm feeling ill.
man: Maybe I can help you. Tell me about your illness.
woman: I woke up this morning with a bad headache.
man: If anyone could tell you about headaches it is me.
woman: And it got even worse. My stomach began to ache, I vomitted and now I'm feeling a little feverish.
man: Would you like me to call an ambulance?
woman: No, no, I think it will do if you thoroughly examine me and give me a prescription.
man: Oh, I can't do that.
woman: Why not? I need some medicine! What kind of damned doctor are you? I have severe pains all over my body and it's getting worse by the minute.
man: Well, I'm sorry but I'm not a doctor. The doctor's surgery is next door.
woman: Why didn't you tell me when I came in?
man: Tell you what?
woman: That you're not the doctor!
man: You didn't ask.

| | |
|---:|:---|
| disease | **Krankheit** |
| stomach | **Magen** |
| feverish | **fiebrig** |
| to examine | **untersuchen** |
| medicine | **Medizin** |

*Dialoge*

## Knapp daneben

Eine Frau betritt eine Praxis.

Frau: Guten Morgen.
Mann: Guten Morgen. Kommen Sie herein und nehmen Sie Platz.
Frau: Ich komme zu Ihnen, weil ich mich krank fühle.
Mann: Vielleicht kann ich Ihnen helfen. Erzählen Sie von Ihrer Krankheit.
Frau: Ich bin heute Morgen aufgewacht und hatte arge Kopfschmerzen.
Mann: Wenn Ihnen irgendjemand etwas über Kopfschmerzen sagen kann, dann bin ich das.
Frau: Und es wurde noch schlimmer. Ich bekam Bauchschmerzen, ich musste mich übergeben und jetzt fühle ich mich fiebrig.
Mann: Soll ich einen Krankenwagen rufen?
Frau: Nein, nein, ich glaube es reicht, wenn Sie mich gründlich untersuchen und mir ein Medikamentenrezept ausstellen.
Mann: Oh, das kann ich nicht machen.
Frau: Warum nicht? Ich brauche ein Medikament. Was für eine verdammte Art von Arzt sind Sie? Ich habe überall große Schmerzen und es wird jede Minute schlimmer.
Mann: Nein, tut mir leid. Ich bin kein Arzt. Die Arztpraxis ist nebenan.
Frau: Warum haben Sie das nicht gesagt, als ich herein kam?
Mann: Ihnen was gesagt?
Frau: Dass Sie gar kein Arzt sind.
Mann: Sie haben mich nicht danach gefragt.

*Arzt*

## A  Kreuzworträtsel

Übersetzen sie die unten angegebenen Wörter ins Englische und setzen Sie diese den Nummern entsprechend ein!

1  sich *übel* fühlen
2  Medikament
3  Krankenhaus
4  Mein Bauch *schmerzt*
5  krank
6  Medikamentenrezept
7  Kopfschmerz
8  untersuchen
9  Tabletten

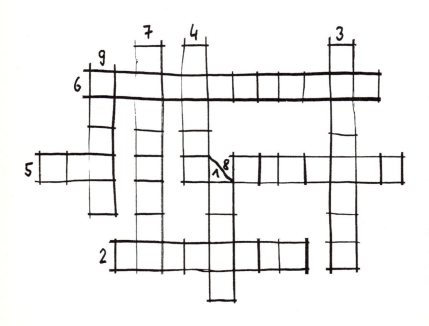

*Dialoge*

## B  Ein Rätsel!

A father and his son had a bad accident in their car. Both were badly injured and brought to hospital.
The surgeon comes in to examine the boy and seeing him cries out:
"Oh God, it's my son!"

Wie kann das sein?

Lösungen Seite 115

## 6  Apotheke

**It takes a child to point out the truth**

A father and his little daughter enter the chemist's.

chemist: Good afternoon. What can I do for you?
man: I sneeze all the time. I think I need something for the flu.
chemist: Yes, just a moment. In my opinion you should take some of these vitamin pills and this cure for influenza.
man: Thank you very much.
chemist: Have you got any pains? Then you should also buy this pain-reliever.
man: No, no pains.
daughter: But I've got pains. I've got stomach ache.
man: That's because your stomach is empty. You would feel better if you had something in it.

A woman comes in.

chemist: Good afternoon, Ms Smithers. How are you?
woman: Good afternoon, Mr Lovejoy. I'm not too well and need some pain-relievers. I have suffered all day from a severe headache.
daughter: That is because it's empty. You'd feel much better, if you had something in it.

| | |
|---:|---|
| prophylaxis | **Prophylaxe** |
| cure | **Heilmittel** |
| flu | **Grippe** |
| pain | **Schmerzen** |
| opinion | **Meinung** |
| empty | **leer** |

*Dialoge*

# Kindermund tut Wahrheit kund

Ein Vater und seine kleine Tochter betreten eine Apotheke.

Apotheker: Guten Tag. Was kann ich für Sie tun?
Vater: Ich niese die ganze Zeit. Ich glaube, ich brauche etwas Vorbeugendes gegen Grippe.
Apotheker: Ja, einen Moment. Meiner Ansicht nach sollten Sie einige dieser Vitamintabletten nehmen und dieses Mittel gegen Erkältungskrankheiten.
Vater: Haben Sie vielen Dank.
Apotheker: Haben Sie Schmerzen? Dann sollten Sie auch ein Schmerzmittel kaufen.
Vater: Nein, keine Schmerzen.
Tochter: Aber ich habe Schmerzen. Ich habe Bauchschmerzen.
Vater: Das liegt daran, dass er leer ist. Du würdest dich besser fühlen, wenn etwas darin wäre.

Eine Frau kommt herein.

Apotheker: Guten Tag, Frau Smithers. Wie geht's?
Frau: Guten Tag, Herr Lovejoy. Es geht mir nicht so gut. Ich brauche ein Schmerzmittel. Ich leide schon den ganzen Tag unter starken Kopfschmerzen.
Tochter: Das liegt daran, dass er leer ist. Du würdest dich besser fühlen, wenn etwas darin wäre.

## A  Vervollständigen Sie bitte die folgenden Sätze in englischer Sprache!

1. If you catch flu you are always _____ .
2. If your body aches you have got _____ .
3. If your head aches you have got a _____ .
4. If you don't eat enough fruit, you need extra _____ .
5. If you cut your finger you need a _____ .

## B  Bringen Sie bitte die Wörter in die richtige Reihenfolge.

1. pain-reliever/should/a/buy/you.

   _____

2. too/not/I'm/well.

   _____

3. stomach/I've/ache/got.

   _____

4. sneezing/time/I'm/all/the.

   _____

5. vitamin/some/these/of/take/pills.

   _____

**C  Kreuzen Sie bitte die richtige Antwort an!**

1. You want to buy a cure, so you go to the
 - [ ] greengrocer's
 - [ ] supermarket
 - [ ] chemist's

2. You have got flu. You should take
 - [ ] a cigarette
 - [ ] pains
 - [ ] a cure
 - [ ] a drink

3. You have got pains. You should take
 - [ ] it easy
 - [ ] a prophylaxis
 - [ ] a pain reliever
 - [ ] a shower

## 7  Post

### I had it on my tongue

A woman enters the post office and walks over to the counter.

| | |
|---|---|
| assistant: | Good morning, Madam. |
| woman: | Good morning. I need ten envelopes for letters and ten postcards, please. |
| assistant: | Yes, of course. Here you are. Anything else? |
| woman: | A sheet of stamps, please. |
| assistant: | Here they are. |
| woman: | When is the next collection? |
| assistant: | The postman has already been here, Madam, but you can leave your letters and cards right here. |
| woman: | That's nice of you. I'll just put the letters in the envelopes and put the addresses on and then I'll come back. |
| assistant: | Okay. See you! |

After twenty minutes the woman comes back and hands over the letters.

| | |
|---|---|
| assistant: | You've forgotten to put the address of the sender on this one. And this letter lacks an address. |
| woman: | Oh, I'm really sorry. I'll correct these mistakes. |
| assistant: | The scales say that this parcel weighs too much. You'll have to put another stamp on it. |
| woman: | Yes, I will. And there was something else. I had it on the tip of my tongue and now it's gone. |
| assistant: | Just think hard and it'll come back to you. |
| woman: | That won't bring it back. It was a 19 p. stamp. |

*Dialoge*

## Es lag mir auf der Zunge

Eine Frau betritt die Post und geht zum Schalter.

| | |
|---|---|
| Beamter: | Guten Morgen. |
| Frau: | Guten Morgen. Ich brauche zehn Briefumschläge und zehn Postkarten. |
| Beamter: | Ja, natürlich. Hier, bitte schön. Noch etwas? |
| Frau: | Einen Bogen Briefmarken, bitte. |
| Beamter: | Hier sind sie. |
| Frau: | Wann ist die nächste Leerung? |
| Beamter: | Der Postbote war schon hier, aber Sie können Ihre Briefe und Postkarten auch hier lassen. |
| Frau: | Das ist nett von Ihnen. Ich stecke nur schnell die Briefe in die Umschläge und schreibe die Adressen darauf und dann komme ich wieder. |
| Beamter: | Gut. Bis gleich. |

Nach zwanzig Minuten kommt die Frau wieder und händigt die Briefe aus.

| | |
|---|---|
| Beamter: | Sie haben vergessen, den Absender auf diesen hier zu schreiben. Und bei diesem fehlt die Adresse. |
| Frau: | Oh, das tut mir sehr leid. Ich werde diese Fehler korrigieren. |
| Beamter: | Die Waage gibt an, dass dieses Paket zu viel wiegt. Sie müssen noch eine Briefmarke dazu kleben. |
| Frau: | Ja, das mache ich. Und da war noch etwas. Ich hatte es auf der Zunge und jetzt ist es weg. |
| Beamter: | Denken Sie mal nach, dann kommt es wieder. |
| Frau: | Das wird nichts helfen. Es war eine 19-p.-Marke. |

**Übersetzen Sie bitte die unten aufgeführten Wörter ins Englische und setzen Sie diese nach den angegebenen Zahlen in das Kreuzworträtsel ein!**

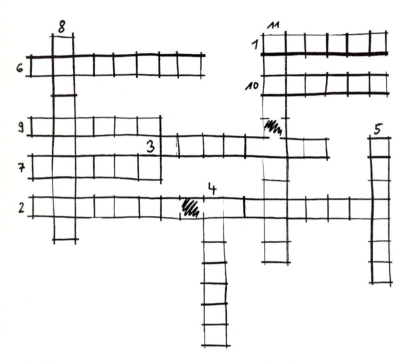

1 Paket
2 Schalterbeamter/in
3 Briefumschlag
4 Adresse
5 Briefträger/in
6 Postkarte
7 Briefmarken
8 Leerung
9 Brief
10 Waage
11 Post

## 8 Supermarkt

### Like mother like son

A woman and her son enter the supermarket.

woman: We need two bottles of milk and a dozen eggs. Will you fetch them?
son: Yes, I will. Oh, look at this. It's Yogi - the new yoghurt for kids! Can I have it?
woman: Yes, okay. But only one. We also need some butter cookies. Go and get some.
son: Yes. Oh, Mom, will you also buy this chocolate bar for me? I really like it!
woman: No. You already had your yoghurt. That's enough. But go and see if you can find frozen pizza.
son: Mum, I've seen ice-cream beside the pizza. What about having ice-cream after lunch?
woman: No. It's too expensive. We'll have fruit. Go and get some bananas and apples.
son: Here they are, but I think strawberries taste better. Can we have some strawberries?
woman: Strawberries? It's March now. Strawberries are much too expensive. Please stop asking for luxury goods, will you? What do you think I am? A millionaire?
son: And what do you think I am? An ascetic?

| | |
|---:|:---|
| frozen pizza | **Tiefkühlpizza** |
| millionaire | **Millionär/in** |
| strawberry | **Erdbeere** |
| ascetic | **Asket/in** |
| luxury goods | **Luxusartikel** |

## Wie die Mutter so der Sohn

Eine Frau und ihr Sohn betreten einen Supermarkt.

Frau: Wir brauchen zwei Flaschen Milch und ein Dutzend Eier. Bist du so lieb und holst sie?

Sohn: Ja, das mach ich. Oh, sieh mal dies hier. Das ist Yogi – der neue Joghurt für Kinder! Kann ich welchen haben?

Frau: Ja, aber nur einen. Wir brauchen auch Butterkekse. Geh und hole welche.

Sohn: Mama, willst du mir nicht auch diese Tafel Schokolade kaufen? Die mag ich wirklich gern!

Frau: Nein. Du hast schon deinen Joghurt. Das ist genug. Aber geh mal und suche Tiefkühlpizza.

Sohn: Hier, bitte schön. Ich habe neben der Pizza Eiscreme gesehen. Wollen wir nicht Eiscreme nach dem Mittagessen haben?

Frau: Nein, das ist zu teuer. Wir werden Obst nehmen. Geh und hole einige Bananen und Äpfel.

Sohn: Hier sind sie, aber ich finde, Erdbeeren schmecken viel besser. Wollen wir ein paar Erdbeeren mitnehmen?

Frau: Erdbeeren? Es ist jetzt März. Erdbeeren sind jetzt viel zu teuer. Hör bitte auf, um Luxusartikel zu betteln. Was glaubst du, was ich bin? Eine Millionärin?

Sohn: Und was glaubst du, was ich bin? Ein Asket?

**A Bringen Sie bitte die durcheinander geratenen Satzstücke in die richtige Reihenfolge.**

1. a dozen/we/need/eggs.

2. chocolate bar/we/this/shall/have?

3. goods/don't/for/luxury/ask!

4. ice-cream/about/what?

5. some/go/fetch/you/will/bananas/and?

6. expensive/too/no/is/it!

7. also/some/need/we/lettuce


**B Übersetzen Sie bitte die folgenden Sätze ins Englische.**

1. Wir brauchen noch Milch.

---

2. Das ist zu teuer.

---

3. Wie wäre es hiermit?

---

4. Geh und suche bitte Tiefkühlpizza.

---

## 9 Andenkenladen

### Something real impressing

A tourist enters a souvenir-shop in Scotland.

shop assistant: Good afternoon, Sir. What can I do for you?
tourist: I'm looking for something really special that will remind me of this wonderful journey through Scotland.
shop assistant: Let's see. Oh, what about these bagpipes? They're a little expensive, but you'll have real fun trying to produce sounds with them.
tourist: No, that's not the right thing. A friend of mine already has some. I want something impressive.
shop assistant: Now I know what you mean and I think I have the right thing for you. Look at this!
tourist: What is it?
shop assistant: It's an original celtic brooch and it's more than 2,000 years old.
tourist: Ha, you're lying.
shop assistant: I beg your pardon?
tourist: You're a swindler!
shop assistant: What was that?
tourist: I'm too clever for that. This "what-d'you-call-it" cannot be more than 2,000 years old, because it's only 1998 now! Ha!
shop assistant (quietly to herself): I'm getting sick of this job.

| | |
|---|---|
| **swindler** | **Schwindler/in** |
| **what-d'you-call-it** | **Dings** |

## Etwas wirklich Beeindruckendes

Ein Tourist betritt einen Andenkenladen in Schottland.

Verkäuferin: Guten Tag. Kann ich Ihnen helfen? Was kann ich für Sie tun?
Tourist: Ich suche etwas ganz Besonderes, das mich an diese wundervolle Reise durch Schottland erinnert.
Verkäuferin: Lassen Sie mich überlegen. Oh, wie wäre es mit diesem Dudelsack? Er ist ein bisschen teuer, aber Sie werden sehr viel Spaß bei dem Versuch haben, Töne zu erzeugen.
Tourist: Nein, das ist nicht das Richtige. Ein Freund von mir hat schon einen. Ich möchte etwas Beeindruckendes.
Verkäuferin: Nun weiß ich was Sie meinen und ich glaube, ich habe das Richtige für Sie. Schauen Sie mal hier!
Tourist: Was ist das?
Verkäuferin: Das ist eine echte keltische Brosche und sie ist älter als 2000 Jahre.
Tourist: Ha, Sie lügen.
Verkäuferin: Wie bitte!?
Tourist: Sie sind eine Betrügerin!
Verkäuferin: Wie war das?
Tourist: Dafür bin ich zu raffiniert. Dieses Ding kann nicht älter als 2000 Jahre sein, denn wir haben ja erst 1998! Ha!
Verkäuferin (leise zu sich selbst): Ich hasse diese Arbeit.

## A  Übersetzen Sie bitte ins Englische.

1. Was kann ich für Sie tun?

2. Ich suche etwas Interessantes.

3. Dieses erinnert mich an einen wunderbaren Freund.

4. Wie wäre es hiermit?

___

5. Nein, das ist nicht das Richtige.

___

6. Was ist das?

___

7. Sie sind eine Schwindlerin!

___

## B  Ergänzen Sie bitte den Dialog mit folgenden Wörtern und Phrasen.

**These are bagpipes, already, looking for, know, at, this one, something**

shop assistant: Good afternoon. What can I do for you?

tourist: I'm _____

really interesting.

shop assistant: Look at _____.

tourist: No, I _____ have one.

shop assistant: Now I _____ what you are

looking for. Look _____ these.

tourist: What is it?

shop assistant: _____.

## 10  Restaurant

### The best restaurant in town

Two women in an office are talking together.

Ann: What was your date like with Alan last evening?
Susan: Oh, Alan was very nice, but the restaurant was horrible.
Ann: What happened?
Susan: First of all we didn't get a table, although Alan had ordered one. After an hour we were finally seated and ordered the menu and the wine card. The waiter was in a hurry and there was a mix-up with our order.
Ann: Oh, dear, I hope the meal was good in the end.
Susan: Absolutely not. The soup was cold. The fish was not done; it was half raw and the service was snooty.
Ann: That's a shame.
Susan: Yes, you can say that again. And the food was too expensive. You had to pay through the nose at that restaurant. But by the way, how was your dinner last night?
Ann: Perfect. The service was really attentive, the meal was very good, the room was not crowded with people and it was cheap. I can really recommend it.
Susan: Then tell me, in what restaurant were you at?
Ann: It wasn't a real restaurant. I stayed at home.

| | |
|---:|:---|
| **horrible** | **schrecklich** |
| **finally** | **letztendlich** |
| **mess up** | **Durcheinander** |
| **by the way** | **da wir gerade davon sprechen** |

*Dialoge*

## Das beste Restaurant der Stadt

Zwei Frauen in einem Büro unterhalten sich.

Ann: Wie war denn dein Rendezvous mit Alan gestern Abend?

Susan: Oh, Alan war sehr nett, aber das Restaurant war schrecklich.

Ann: Was ist denn passiert?

Susan: Erstens haben wir keinen Tisch bekommen, obwohl Alan einen bestellt hatte. Nach einer Stunde bekamen wir einen und bestellten die Menükarte und die Weinkarte. Die Bedienung hatte viel zu tun und daher gab es ein Durcheinander mit unserer Bestellung.

Ann: Oh, du Arme, ich hoffe, das Essen war letztendlich gut.

Susan: Überhaupt nicht. Die Suppe war kalt. Der Fisch war nicht gar, sondern halb roh und die Bedienung war arrogant.

Ann: Was für ein Pech.

Susan: Ja, du sagst es. Und das Essen war zu teuer. Ein richtiges Nepplokal war das. Aber da wir gerade davon sprechen, wie war dein Abendessen gestern?

Ann: Großartig. Die Bedienung war sehr aufmerksam, das Essen war sehr gut, der Raum war nicht vollgestopft mit Leuten und es war billig. Ich kann es wirklich weiterempfehlen.

Susan: Dann sag mir doch, in welchem Restaurant du warst.

Ann: Es war kein richtiges Restaurant. Ich bin zu Hause geblieben.

## Ordnen Sie bitte die Satzstücke in Kategorien ein.

the meal was expensive/the fish was good/the service was attentive/the soup was cold/the fish was half raw/the service was snooty/the room was not crowded/the wine tasted good/we didn't get a table/the waiter was in a hurry/one can recommend it/the meal was cheap

Gutes Restaurant:

1. _____
2. _____
3. _____
4. _____
5. _____
6. _____

Schlechtes Restaurant:

1. _____
2. _____
3. _____
4. _____
5. _____
6. _____

## 11  Nachtleben

### A big night out

A woman and a man are looking at the newspaper.

woman: Let's see what we can do this evening. Ah, what about going to the opera?

man: Sounds good! Hanging around at the bar, drinking lager, ...

woman: No, you are thinking of a pub. The opera is like a theatre with the difference that the actors are singing.

man: Oh, I see. I don't think I like operas.

woman: Okay. Here, look. This'll be nice. What about going to the cinema?

man: Yes, that'll be a laugh. Drinking beer, meeting nice people, ...

woman: No, no. What you have in mind is a pub again. In the cinema we'd watch a film and eat popcorn.

man: Hm, that doesn't sound fun. Are there other alternatives?

woman: Yes, of course. Would you like to go to the disco or any kind of music bar?

man: Oh yes, certainly. Drinking dark beer, playing darts, talking to people, ...

woman: You are talking about a pub again. Well, I give up. What about going to the pub this evening?

man: Whatever you want. The main thing is that you have a jolly good time.

woman (aside): Oh dear. What did I do to deserve this loony.

## Ein Abend in der Stadt

Eine Frau und ein Mann sehen in die Zeitung.

Frau: Mal schauen, was wir heute Abend machen können. Ah, wie wäre es mit einem Opernbesuch?

Mann: Hört sich gut an. An der Bar rumsitzen, Bier trinken, ...

Frau: Nein, du denkst an eine Kneipe. Die Oper ist wie ein Theater mit dem Unterschied, dass die Schauspieler singen.

Mann: Oh, ich verstehe. Ich glaube, ich mag keine Opern.

Frau: Also gut. Sieh mal hier. Das wäre nett. Wollen wir nicht ins Kino gehen?

Mann: Ja, das wird ein großer Spaß. Bier trinken, nette Leute treffen, ...

Frau: Nein, nein. Woran du denkst ist eine Kneipe. In einem Kino würden wir einen Film sehen und Popcorn essen.

Mann: Hm, das hört sich nicht besonders lustig an. Gibt es noch andere Alternativen?

Frau: Ja, natürlich. Würdest du gerne in die Disco gehen oder in irgendein anderes Tanzlokal?

Mann: Oh ja, natürlich. Dunkles Bier trinken, Darts spielen, sich mit Leuten unterhalten, ...

Frau: Du redest schon wieder von einer Kneipe. Also, ich gebe auf. Wie wäre es heute Abend mit einem Kneipenbesuch?

Mann: Was auch immer du willst. Hauptsache du amüsierst dich.

Frau (zu sich selbst): Oh je, womit habe ich diesen Blödmann verdient.

## A Kreuzen Sie bitte die richtige Antwort an.

1. What do you call a theatre where the actors are singing?
☐ pub
☐ opera
☐ zoo

2. What do you call a house where people watch movies?
☐ living room
☐ office
☐ cinema

3. What do you call a place where people can dance?
☐ disco
☐ toilet
☐ café
☐ music bar

## B Übersetzen Sie bitte die folgenden Phrasen ins Englische.

1. Wie wäre es mit ...

_____

2. Das wäre ein großer Spaß.

_____

3. Das mag ich wirklich.

_____

Lösungen Seite 118

*Nachtleben*

## 12 Pub

**Another quick one!**

Jack is sitting in his favorite pub. His friend Al is coming in.

Jack: Hi, Al, lovely weather today, isn't it?
Al: Yes, great.
Jack: I haven't seen you for ages. What have you been up to?
Al: It's just... I haven't been out for weeks. Instead of going to the pub, I've been reading books.
Jack.: You are kidding! What's yours?
Al: Oh, that's nice of you. I'll have a lager.

Jack clears a path through the crowd and comes back with two half pints.

Al: Thank you. Cheers.
Jack: Cheers. So then, what kind of books did you read?
Al: I read some guides for daily life. For example "How to impress people" or "Collecting things".
Jack: Those books are useful. Another one?
Al: No, not for me, thank you.

Jack orders another lager at the bar and comes back.

Al: Everyday life has been much more exciting since I have had those books.
Jack: I would like to read them, too. Can you lend me one?
Al: I'm not sure ...
Jack: Is that one in your pocket?
Al: I don't think that one will impress you.
publican: Last order at the bar Ladies and Gentlemen!

*Dialoge*

Jack: Just a minute, Al. I'll just fetch another beer and then you'll show it to me, will you?

Jack hurries to the bar for his pint of beer. Then he comes back.

Jack: Now show me. I'm very interested.
Al: You wouldn't like it. It's not the kind of guide you want.
Jack: Why not?
Al: Because it's "Seven weeks without drinking".


**Einige Tipps für einen Besuch im Pub:**

1. Ein Pub ist voller netter Leute
Wenn Sie in einen Pub gehen, sollten Sie darauf vorbereitet sein, von anderen Gästen angesprochen zu werden. Das beste und beliebteste Thema zu Beginn eines Gespräches ist natürlich das Wetter.

2. Wo bleibt der Kellner?
Wenn Sie ein Bier bestellen möchten, dann tun Sie das an der Bar und bezahlen dort auch gleich.

3. „Ich will kein schwarzes, klebriges Bier!"
Es gibt sehr viele verschiedene Biersorten und falls Sie Experimente nicht lieben und ein kühles blondes Pils möchten, dann bestellen Sie am besten ein *lager*. *Lager* gibt es in zwei Größen. *Half pint* entspricht ungefähr 0,3 l und *pint* entspricht ungefähr 0,5 l. Sie sagen dann z. B. *Half a pint of lager, please.*

## Noch ein schnelles Bier

Jack sitzt in seinem Stammlokal. Sein Freund Al betritt den Raum.

Jack: Hallo Al, schönes Wetter heute, was?
Al: Ja, großartig.
Jack: Ich habe dich schon eine ganze Weile nicht mehr gesehen. Wo bist du gewesen?
Al: Es ist nur ... Ich bin wochenlang nicht ausgegangen. Anstatt in die Kneipe zu gehen, habe ich Bücher gelesen.
Jack: Du machst Witze! Ein Bier?
Al: Oh, das ist sehr nett von dir. Ich nehme ein Lager.

Jack bahnt sich seinen Weg durch die Menge und kommt mit zwei kleinen Bieren wieder.

Al: Danke schön. Prost.
Jack: Prost. Welche Art von Büchern hast du gelesen?
Al: Ich habe ein paar Ratgeber für das tägliche Leben gelesen. Zum Beispiel „Wie beeindruckt man andere" oder „Sachen sammeln".
Jack: Solche Bücher sind nützlich. Noch ein Bier?
Al: Nein, für mich nicht, danke.

Jack bestellt noch ein Lager an der Bar und kommt wieder.

Al: Der Alltag ist viel interessanter, seit ich diese Bücher habe.
Jack: Ich würde sie auch gerne lesen. Kannst du mir eines leihen?
Al: Ich bin mir nicht sicher ...
Jack: Ist das da eines in deiner Tasche?
Al: Ich glaube nicht, dass dieses Buch dich beeindrucken wird.

Wirt: Letzte Bestellung an der Theke!
Jack: Eine Sekunde, Al. Ich hol nur schnell ein neues Bier und dann zeigst du mir dein Buch, ja?

Jack eilt zur Bar, um ein großes Bier zu holen. Dann kommt er wieder zurück.

Jack: Jetzt zeig es mir. Ich bin sehr neugierig.
Al: Du wirst es nicht mögen. Es ist nicht die Art von Ratgeber, die du magst.
Jack: Wieso nicht?
Al: Weil es „Sieben Wochen ohne Alkohol" heißt.

## Übersetzen Sie bitte den folgenden Dialog ins Englische.

1. Tom: Hallo Bill. Wie geht's?
2. Bill: Hallo Tom. Mir geht's gut, und dir?
3. Tom: Danke, gut. Schönes Wetter heute, was?
4. Bill: Ja, großartig.
5. Tom: Ein Bier?
6. Bill: Das ist nett von dir. Ich nehme ein Lager.
7. Tom: Was für ein Buch hast du in der Tasche?
8. Bill: Es ist ein Ratgeber.
9. Tom: Den würde ich auch gerne einmal lesen.
10. Bill: Hier, bitte schön.

1. _____
2. _____
3. _____
4. _____
5. _____
6. _____
7. _____
8. _____
9. _____
10. _____

## 13  Getränke bestellen

### Some things need a little time

Andy and Janette are sitting in a café.

Andy: I'm not hungry. I think I'll just have a drink.
Janette: I'm very thirsty. Please give me the list of beverages, will you?
Andy: Shall we have something alcoholic? I'd like to have a glass of white wine.
Janette: No, not for me. I had a hangover yesterday. I want to keep a clear head. Wine doesn't agree with me.
waiter: Good afternoon. Would you like anything to drink?
Andy: White wine for me, please.
Janette: I'd like some orange juice, please.
waiter: Oh, I'm really sorry, but we are out of orange juice.
Janette: I'll take mineral water, then.
waiter: Yes, white wine and mineral water, thank you.
Andy: What did you drink that caused the hangover?
Janette: We first had sparkling wine. Later I drank brown ale. It made me feel a bit tipsy, but I wasn't drunk. Maybe I should not have had whisky, or was it gin? I don't know.
Andy: You'd better control your alcohol consumption.
Janette: Yes, Mr. Know-all. I'm thirsty. (to the waiter) Excuse me, but do we have to sit here until we die of thirst?
Waiter: No, Madam, we close at eight.

| | |
|---:|---|
| hangover | Kater |
| sparkling wine | Sekt |
| Mr. Know-all | Besserwisser |

## Manches braucht seine Zeit

Andy und Janette sitzen in einem Café.

Andy: Ich habe keinen Hunger. Ich glaube, ich möchte nur ein Getränk.
Janette: Ich bin sehr durstig. Gib mir doch bitte mal die Getränkekarte.
Andy: Wollen wir etwas Alkoholisches trinken? Ich hätte gerne ein Glas Weißwein.
Janette: Nein, für mich nicht. Ich hatte gestern einen Kater. Ich möchte einen klaren Kopf behalten. Wein bekommt mir nicht.
Kellner: Guten Tag. Möchten Sie etwas zu trinken bestellen?
Andy: Für mich bitte Weißwein.
Janette: Ich hätte gerne einen Orangensaft.
Kellner: Oh, das tut mir leid, aber der Orangensaft ist aus.
Janette: Dann nehme ich Mineralwasser.
Kellner: Ja, Weißwein und Mineralwasser, danke schön.
Andy: Was hast du denn getrunken, das den Kater verursachte?
Janette: Wir haben zuerst Sekt getrunken. Später hatte ich dunkles Bier. Ich hatte einen kleinen Schwips, aber ich war nicht betrunken. Ich hätte wohl nicht den Whisky trinken sollen, oder war es Gin? Ich weiß es nicht.
Andy: Du solltest deinen Alkoholkonsum besser kontrollieren.
Janette: Ja, du Besserwisser. Ich habe Durst.
(zur Bedienung:) Entschuldigung, aber müssen wir hier sitzen, bis wir verdurstet sind?
Kellner: Nein, wir schließen um acht.

**Übersetzen Sie bitte die Sätze ins Englische.**

1. Gib mir bitte die Getränkeliste.

2. Ich habe Durst.

3. Ich hätte gerne etwas Alkoholisches.

4. Ich habe einen Kater.

5. Ich möchte einen klaren Kopf behalten.

6. Alkohol bekommt mir nicht.

7. Ich hatte einen Schwips.

8. Ich war nicht betrunken.

9. Tut mir leid, das Mineralwasser ist aus.

## 14 Wetter

**What was the weather like?**

Agatha and Christine meet in a café.

Agatha: Hello Christine, great to see you.
Christine: Hi, Agatha. I haven't seen you for over two weeks. Have you been on holiday?
Agatha: Yes, let's sit down and I'll tell you. I've been in Denmark. I went on the ferry and there was a real storm during the crossing. I got seasick.
Christine: Oh, how silly.
Agatha: It was a thunderstorm with thunder and lightning. When it ended we could see a wonderful rainbow across the sky.
Christine: And in Denmark? I hope the weather was better there.
Agatha: When we reached Denmark the sun was shining. Not one cloud in two weeks. It was always a little windy at the seaside.
Christine: That sounds good.
Agatha: In my opinion it was too hot. One couldn't sleep at night because of the heat, but what was the weather like here in Warwick?
Christine: The same as always, typical English weather. Foggy in the morning or at least misty. Clouds and sometimes rain. It wasn't cold but it also wasn't warm.
Agatha: I really love that kind of weather. One can count on the unsettled weather in Britain.

| | |
|---|---|
| **ferry** | **Fähre** |
| **seasick** | **seekrank** |

## Wie war das Wetter?

Agatha und Christine treffen sich in einem Café.

Agatha: Hallo Christine, nett dich zu sehen.
Christine: Hallo Agatha. Ich habe dich schon zwei Wochen lang nicht gesehen. Warst du auf Reisen?
Agatha: Ja, setz dich und dann erzähle ich es dir. Ich war in Dänemark. Ich bin mit der Fähre gefahren und während der Fahrt gab es einen richtigen Sturm. Ich wurde seekrank.
Christine: Oh, wie dumm.
Agatha: Es war ein Gewitter mit Donner und Blitzen. Als es vorbei war, konnten wir einen wundervollen Regenbogen am Himmel sehen.
Christine: Und in Dänemark? Ich hoffe, das Wetter war dort besser.
Agatha: Als wir Dänemark erreichten, schien die Sonne. Zwei Wochen lang keine Wolke. An der See war es immer ein bisschen windig.
Christine: Das hört sich gut an.
Agatha: Meiner Meinung nach war es zu heiß. Man konnte nachts wegen der Hitze nicht schlafen. Aber wie war das Wetter hier in Warwick?
Christine: Wie immer. Typisches, englisches Wetter. Neblig am Morgen oder zumindest diesig. Viele Wolken und manchmal hat es geregnet. Es war nicht kalt, aber es war auch nicht warm.
Agatha: Ich liebe diese Art von Wetter. Man kann sich in England auf die Unbeständigkeit des Wetters verlassen.

**A Übersetzen Sie bitte die in Klammern stehenden Wörter ins Englische und setzen Sie diese in die Lücken ein.**

1. It's _____ (sonnig). The. _____ (Sonne) is _____ (scheint).
2. It's a little _____ (wolkig). There are _____ (Wolken) in the sky.
3. Tomorrow there will be a _____ (Gewitter) with _____ (Donner) and _____ (Blitz).
4. After that it will _____ (regnen).
5. In the morning it will be _____ (neblig) or at least _____ (diesig).
6. That's an _____ (unbeständig) kind of weather.

**B Ergänzen Sie bitte die Sätze. Achten Sie auf die Wettersymbole zu jedem Satz!**

What's the weather like?

1. It's _____

2. It's _____

3. It's _____

4. It's _____

5. It's _____

Lösungen Seite 120

## 15  Nach dem Weg fragen

**How to walk on the garden path**

A woman is walking along in a town and starts talking to a man sitting in a car.

woman: Excuse me, Sir, could you tell me the way to the Museum of Modern Arts?
man: Certainly. Keep going straight on for the next hundred yards, then turn left at the traffic lights.
woman: Then I'll be at Stanton's Corner, right?
man: Yes, and then straight ahead again for about fifty yards. At the roundabout you turn right, but you have to go through the subway.
woman: There is a church.
man: Yes, there is. Go round the church and turn right again. Go straight on until you see the river, then turn left again.
woman: Before or after passing the river?
man: Before passing it. You will be at the Goose Market, a very nice square, cross it and turn left.
woman: That sounds like a long way to go.
man: It will take you about half an hour, but listen, keep on going through King's Road and cross three other streets, then turn left and the very next you have to turn right, ...
woman: Stop. This town is not that large. There must be a shorter way to the Museum.
man: Yes, maybe, but I don't know it. I'm a taxi driver.

| | |
|---:|:---|
| subway | **Fußgängerunterführung** |
| roundabout | **Kreisverkehr** |
| very next | **gleich die nächste** |

*Dialoge*

## Wie man den längsten Weg wählt

Eine Frau geht in einer Stadt spazieren und beginnt ein Gespräch mit einem Mann, der in einem Auto sitzt.

Frau: Entschuldigen Sie bitte, können Sie mir den Weg zum Museum für moderne Kunst erklären?
Mann: Natürlich. Gehen Sie etwa 100 Yards geradeaus. Dann biegen Sie an der Ampel links ab.
Frau: Dann bin ich am Stanton's Corner, oder?
Mann: Ja, und dann wieder geradeaus etwa 50 Yards. Beim Kreisverkehr biegen Sie rechts ab, aber Sie müssen durch die Fußgängerunterführung gehen.
Frau: Da ist eine Kirche.
Mann: Ja. Gehen Sie um die Kirche herum und biegen Sie wieder rechts ab. Gehen Sie geradeaus, bis Sie den Fluss sehen. Biegen Sie dann wieder links ab.
Frau: Bevor oder nachdem ich den Fluss überquert habe?
Mann: Bevor Sie ihn überqueren. Sie sind dann am Geese Market. Sehr schöner Platz. Überqueren Sie ihn und biegen Sie links ab.
Frau: Das scheint ein sehr langer Weg zu sein.
Mann: Sie benötigen dafür ungefähr eine halbe Stunde, aber hören Sie weiter. Gehen Sie weiter durch die King's Road und überqueren Sie drei andere Straßen. Dann biegen Sie links ab und gleich bei der nächsten biegen Sie rechts ab, ...
Frau: Aufhören. Diese Stadt ist nicht so groß. Es muss einen kürzeren Weg zu dem Museum geben.
Mann: Ja vielleicht, aber ich kenne ihn nicht. Ich bin Taxifahrer.

**A  Beschreiben Sie bitte den Weg, der auf der gegenüberliegenden Seite dargestellt wird.**

---
---
---
---
---
---
---

crossing with traffic light (1)  
cinema (2)  
bank (3)  
church (4)  
theatre (5)  

museum (6)  
chemist's (7)  
supermarket (8)  
park (9)  

**B  Folgen Sie der nachfolgenden Wegbeschreibung anhand der Karte. Wohin führt sie?**

You are in a park. Go to the church and go round the church on the left hand side. There is a cinema. Turn left and follow the road to the traffic lights. Turn left. Go straight ahead until the road ends. Turn left again and go straight ahead. There you are.

*Nach dem Weg fragen* 63

# 16 Auto

**You are a real expert, John!**

John is sitting in a café and waiting for a friend to come. Helen is just entering.

John: How are you, Helen?
Helen: Thanks, I'm fine. And you?
John: It could be worse.
Helen: What has happened?
John: I had an accident yesterday. My car is at the garage, and I had to hire another one for a short time.
Helen: I hope the car was okay. One can never be sure with hire cars. Everything seems fine and when you leave the garage, the problems start.
John: To be on the safe side, I checked it.
Helen: Did you check the oil and the tyre pressure?
John: Yes, of course. I also checked the head lights and the engine.
Helen: You're an expert.
John: I would have checked the car even more, but I was in a hurry, because of you waiting here.
Helen: But I haven't been waiting. When I came in, you were already here. How did you manage to get here that quickly?
John: It wasn't anything to do with me. The brakes were out of order.

| | |
|---:|:---|
| garage | Werkstatt |
| to hire | mieten |
| tyre pressure | Luftdruck |
| head lights | Scheinwerfer |
| brakes | Bremsen |

## Du bist ein echter Experte, John!

John sitzt in einem Café und wartet auf eine Freundin. Helen kommt gerade herein.

John: Wie geht's, Helen?
Helen: Danke, gut. Und dir?
John: Es könnte schlimmer sein.
Helen: Was ist passiert?
John: Ich hatte gestern einen Unfall. Mein Auto ist in der Werkstatt und ich musste für die kurze Zeit ein anderes Auto mieten.
Helen: Ich hoffe, das Auto war in Ordnung. Bei Mietautos kann man nie wissen. Meistens machen sie einen guten Eindruck und wenn man die Werkstatt verlässt, kommen die Probleme.
John: Sicherheitshalber habe ich es überprüft.
Helen: Hast du den Ölstand und den Luftdruck gemessen?
John: Ja, natürlich. Ich habe auch die Scheinwerfer und den Motor überprüft.
Helen: Du bist ein Experte.
John: Ich hätte das Auto noch ein bisschen länger überprüft, aber ich hatte es eilig, weil du hier auf mich gewartet hast.
Helen: Aber ich habe nicht gewartet. Als ich reinkam, warst du schon hier. Wie hast du es angestellt, so schnell hierher zu kommen?
John: Es lag nicht an mir. Die Bremse war kaputt.

## A  Ordnen Sie bitte die Wörter in den Aussagen so, dass ein sinnvoller Dialog entsteht.

man: want/car/to/hire/I /a.
woman: about/one/this/what?
man: don't/a/I/want/cadillac.
woman: at/then/look/this.
man: tire/have/check/the/pressure/I/to.
woman: pressure/tire/the/okay/is.
man: have/check/oil/I/to/the.
woman: oil/also/the/is/okay.
man: like/colour/that/I/the/don't/of/car.
woman: should/a/you/hire/bicycle.

man: _____

woman: _____

man: _____

woman: _____

man: _____

woman: _____

man: _____

woman: _____

man: _____

woman: _____

## B  Scherzfrage:

What do tunas call car drivers?
(Wie nennen Thunfische Autofahrer/Autofahrerinnen?)

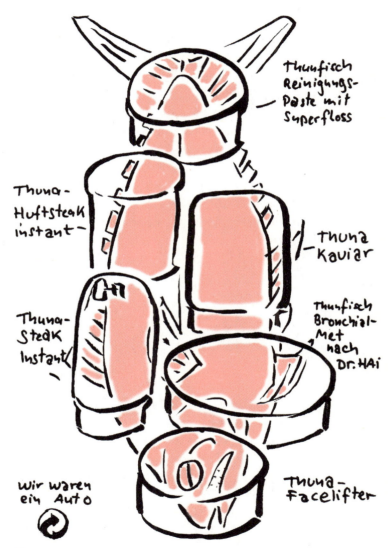

## 17  Fremdenverkehrsbüro

### Home sweet home

A man enters the tourist information office.

man: Good morning, Madam.
woman: Good morning, Sir. Can I help you.
man: I need some information about this town. I want to know all about the sights one can see here.
woman: There are many interesting sights in our town and I am sure that you will spend a wonderful time here. If you are interested in churches, you should visit our cathedral.
man: I saw this small cathedral when I arrived yesterday. It wasn't too impressive. We have a much bigger cathedral in the town where I live. It's the oldest cathedral one has ever seen.
woman: Then you shouldn't miss visiting our castle near the city at the top of the hill. You will like it.
man: There are two castles in the town where I live. Queen Victoria visited one of them once and the other one is well-known for its famous rose garden.
woman: Er, this must be a really lovely place. If you like gardens, you should visit our park. It is surrounded by a small river and you can swim there.
man: I don't want to swim here. I swim every day when I am at home. There is a river next to my house and it is absolutely beautiful.
woman: I see. What about our museum. There is a collection of Modern Arts. We have some pictures by famous painters.

man: You should see the Museum of Modern Arts in my town! It's fantastic! Hundreds of pictures by famous painters from all over the world.

woman: Very interesting. ... Er, I could offer you a ticket for our theatre. There will be a Shakespeare play this evening, but I think you have seen it already in your town.

man: I have seen all Shakespeare plays in our theatre. We always have famous guest actors there.

woman: Just one question! Has there been a big fire in your town that destroyed everything?

man: No. There wasn't a fire.

woman: Has there been a disease in your town? Maybe the plague?

man: Pardon? The plague?

woman: Has there been an invasion of unknown flying objects?

man: Unknown flying objects?? Why are you asking this stupid question?

woman: I'm just wondering why you left your fantastic town. There must be an urgent reason. Or what is it that makes you stay in our ugly town?

man: ???

| | |
|---:|:---|
| sight | Sehenswürdigkeit |
| cathedral | Kathedrale |
| castle | Burg |
| surrounded | umgeben |
| famous | berühmt |
| disease | Krankheit |
| plague | Pest |
| invasion | Invasion |
| unknown flying objects | UFO |
| urgent reason | zwingender Grund |

## Heimat, süße Heimat

Ein Mann betritt das Fremdenverkehrsbüro.

Mann: Guten Morgen.
Frau: Guten Morgen. Kann ich etwas für Sie tun?
Mann: Ich brauche einige Informationen über diese Stadt. Ich will alles über die Sehenswürdigkeiten wissen, die man hier ansehen kann.
Frau: Es gibt in unserer Stadt viele interessante Sehenswürdigkeiten und ich bin sicher, dass Sie hier eine schöne Zeit verbringen werden. Wenn Sie an Kirchen interessiert sind, sollten Sie unsere Kathedrale besuchen.
Mann: Ich habe diese kleine Kathedrale gestern gesehen als ich hier eintraf. In der Stadt, in der ich lebe, haben wir eine viel größere Kathedrale. Es ist die älteste Kathedrale, die man jemals gesehen hat.
Frau: Dann sollten Sie einen Besuch unserer Burg nahe der Stadt auf einem Hügel gelegen nicht versäumen. Sie werden es mögen.
Mann: In der Stadt, in der ich lebe, gibt es zwei Burgen. Königin Victoria besuchte die eine einmal und die andere ist bekannt durch ihren Rosengarten.
Frau: Äh, das muss wirklich ein schönes Plätzchen sein. Wenn Sie Gärten mögen, sollten Sie unseren Park besuchen. Er ist von einem kleinen Fluss umgeben und Sie können dort auch schwimmen.
Mann: Ich will hier nicht schwimmen. Ich schwimme zu Hause jeden Tag. Neben meinem Haus ist ein unheimlich schöner Fluss.
Frau: Ich verstehe. Wie wäre es mit unserem Museum? Es gibt dort eine Sammlung moderner Kunst.

| | Einige Bilder stammen von berühmten Malern. |
|---|---|
| Mann: | Sie sollten das Museum der modernen Künste in meiner Stadt mal sehen! Es ist großartig. Hunderte von Bildern der berühmtesten Maler aus aller Welt. |
| Frau: | Sehr interessant. ... Äh, ich könnte Ihnen eine Theaterkarte anbieten. Heute Abend wird ein Shakespeare Stück gegeben, aber ich nehme mal an, Sie haben es bereits in Ihrer Stadt gesehen. |
| Mann: | Ich habe alle Shakespeare Stücke in unserem Theater gesehen. Wir haben immer berühmte Gastschauspieler. |
| Frau: | Eine Frage! Gab es in ihrer Stadt ein Feuer, das alles zerstörte? |
| Mann: | Nein, da war kein Feuer. |
| Frau: | Gab es eine Kankheit? Vielleicht die Pest? |
| Mann: | Wie bitte? Die Pest? |
| Frau: | Gab es eine UFO-Invasion? |
| Mann: | UFOs?? Warum stellen Sie so dumme Fragen? |
| Frau: | Ich frage mich nur, warum Sie Ihre fantastische Stadt verlassen haben. Es muss doch einen dringenden Grund gehabt haben. Oder was veranlasst Sie, in unserer hässlichen Stadt zu bleiben? |
| Mann: | ??? |

**Beantworten Sie bitte die folgenden Fragen.**

Jede Zahl unter dem einzusetzenden Lösungswort steht für einen betimmten Buchstaben. Finden Sie die Buchstaben heraus und ordnen Sie diese den Zahlen zu. Je mehr Buchstaben Sie herausfinden, umso leichter wird das Erraten der gesuchten Wörter.

1 =         6 =         11 =

2 =         7 =         12 =

3 =         8 =         13 =

4 =         9 =

5 =         10 =

1. How do you call a house where you can see pieces of art?

   _____
   3  5  1  7  5  3

2. How do you call a big garden in the middle of a town?

   _____
   2  4  6  8

3. How do you call a house where you can see actors?

   _____
   10  9  7  4  10  6  7

4. How do you call a big church?

   _____
   11  4  10  9  7  12  6  4  13

5. How do you call a house where kings and queens live in?

   _____
   11  4  1  10  13  7

72     *Dialoge*                     Lösungen Seite 121

## 18  Bahnhof

### On the move

A woman at the station walks over to the ticket office.

clerk: Good morning, Madam. Can I help you?
woman: What's the second class fare to Leeds, please?
clerk: Single or return, Madam?
woman: Return, please.
clerk: It's seven pounds.
woman: I don't have to change, do I?
clerk: Yes you have to change in Sheffield.
woman: Could you tell me when the next train to Leeds is and when it arrives?
clerk: It leaves in about ten minutes and will be in Leeds at half past four.
woman: How long is the wait in Sheffield?
clerk: It's about an hour, Madam.
woman: Do I have to reserve a seat?
clerk: No, you needn't reserve a seat.
woman: I'm not in the mood for sitting around at a strange station for an hour. It's such a bore.
clerk: If I were you, I would take the bus. It is faster and you don't have to wait for your connection.
woman: That's a good idea. I really don't know how to thank you for your advice.
clerk: Since the invention of money by the Phoenicians, this question has actually become unnecessary, Madam ...
woman: Hm. I see.

**mood    Stimmung**

## Unterwegs

Eine Frau auf dem Bahnhof geht zum Schalter.

Beamter: Guten Morgen. Kann ich Ihnen helfen?
Frau: Wie teuer ist eine Fahrkarte zweiter Klasse nach Leeds?
Beamter: Einfach oder hin und zurück?
Frau: Hin und zurück, bitte.
Beamter: Sie kostet sieben Pfund.
Frau: Ich muss doch nicht umsteigen, oder?
Beamter: Doch, Sie müssen in Sheffield umsteigen.
Frau: Wann fährt der nächste Zug nach Leeds und wann kommt er dort an?
Beamter: Er fährt in ungefähr zehn Minuten und kommt um halb fünf in Leeds an.
Frau: Wie lange dauert der Aufenthalt in Sheffield?
Beamter: Ungefähr eine Stunde.
Frau: Soll ich lieber einen Platz reservieren lassen?
Beamter: Nein, Sie brauchen keinen Platz reservieren zu lassen.
Frau: Ich habe keine Lust eine Stunde auf einem fremden Bahnhof herumzusitzen. Es ist langweilig.
Beamter: Wenn ich Sie wäre, würde ich den Bus nehmen. Er ist schneller, und Sie müssen nicht auf einen Anschlusszug warten.
Frau: Das ist eine gute Idee. Ich weiß gar nicht, wie ich Ihnen für diesen guten Rat danken soll.
Beamter: Seit der Erfindung des Geldes durch die Phönizier ist diese Frage eigentlich überflüssig geworden ...
Frau: Hm, ich verstehe.

## A Bringen Sie bitte den durcheinander geratenen Dialog in die richtige Reihenfolge.

1. Return.
2. Do I have to change?
3. What's the second class fare to Dublin?
4. How long do I have to wait for the connection?
5. It's seven pounds, Sir.
6. Good morning, Sir. Can I help you?
7. Single or return?
8. Yes, you will have to change.
9. About two hours.
10. That's far too long. I think I'll take the car.

## B Übersetzen Sie bitte ins Englische.

1. Eine Fahrkarte zweiter Klasse

2. Einfach oder zurück?

3. Wartezeit (auf den Anschlusszug)

4. Anschlusszug

# *Korrespondenz*

## 19  Hotelreservierung

**Fax**

Fax from:       Barbara White
                06823555380

to:             George Hotel, Bath
                960349587930

date:           April 22, 1998
time:           14:03

Dear Sir or Madam,

This summer my husband and I want to spend our holiday in Bath from 13th August until the 20th.
So I'd like to book a half-board double room with bath, toilet, TV set and telephone. We would like to have a quiet room with a sea view and a balcony as shown in your brochure. Would you be so kind as to tell me what you charge for a room?
If you don't have the required accommodation at this time, I would like you to inform me about other hotels in Bath.

                                          Yours faithfully,
                                          Barbara White

**Fax**

| | |
|---|---|
| Fax von: | Barbara White |
| | 06823555380 |
| an: | George Hotel, Bath |
| | 960349587930 |
| Datum: | 22.4.1998 |
| Uhrzeit: | 14:03 |

Sehr geehrte Damen und Herren,

mein Mann und ich möchten unseren Urlaub vom
13. bis zum 20. August in diesem Sommer gerne in Bath verbringen.
Daher möchte ich ein Doppelzimmer mit Halbpension reservieren lassen mit einem Bad, einer Toilette, einem Fernseher und einem Telefon. Wir hätten gerne ein ruhiges Zimmer mit Seeblick und einem Balkon, wie in Ihrem Prospekt angegeben. Seien Sie so nett und sagen Sie mir, was Sie für ein Zimmer berechnen.
Wenn Sie zu dem Zeitpunkt keine entsprechende Unterkunft haben, informieren Sie mich doch bitte über andere Hotels in Bath.

Mit freundlichen Grüßen
Barbara White

**Answer**

Fax to:      Barbara White
             06823555380

from:        George Hospital
             960349587930

date:        April 22, 1998
time:        18:55

Dear Mrs. White,

I'm very glad to hear that you and your husband are going to visit our nice town. I'm very sorry, but we don't have double rooms for couples. It is not allowed to mix up the sexes in our house. I could offer you a room with two other women and your husband could book a room with several other men. I think that would not be the kind of quiet accommodation you are looking for.
We also don't offer half-board, because our guests are normally not allowed to leave the house. I think you got the wrong fax number: this is not a hotel but a hospital. There are several nice hotels in this town.
Please contact the tourist information office for more information.

                                              Yours,
                                              Dr. West

| | |
|---|---|
| couples | **Paare** |
| to mix up | **vermischen** |
| sexes | **Geschlechter** |

**Antwort**

Fax an:        Barbara White
               06823555380

von:           George Hospital
               960349587930

Datum:         22.4.1998
Uhrzeit:       18:55


Sehr geehrte Frau White,

ich freue mich zu hören, dass Sie und Ihr Mann unsere schöne Stadt besuchen wollen. Es tut mir sehr leid, aber wir haben keine Doppelzimmer für Paare. Es ist in unserem Haus nicht erlaubt, die Geschlechter gemeinsam unterzubringen. Ich könnte Ihnen ein Zimmer mit zwei anderen Frauen anbieten und Ihr Mann könnte ein Zimmer mit diversen anderen Männern buchen. Ich glaube, das ist nicht die Art von ruhiger Unterkunft, die Sie suchen.
Wir haben auch keine Zimmer mit Halbpension, denn unsere Gäste dürfen normalerweise das Haus nicht verlassen. Ich glaube, Sie haben die falsche Faxnummer, denn dies hier ist gar kein Hotel, sondern ein Krankenhaus.
Es gibt viele schöne Hotels in dieser Stadt. Für mehr Informationen setzen Sie sich doch bitte mit dem Fremdenverkehrsbüro in Verbindung.

Mit freundlichen Grüßen
Dr. West

**Übersetzen Sie bitte die unten angegebenen Wörter ins Englische und tragen Sie diese den Zahlen entsprechend in das Kreuzworträtsel ein.**

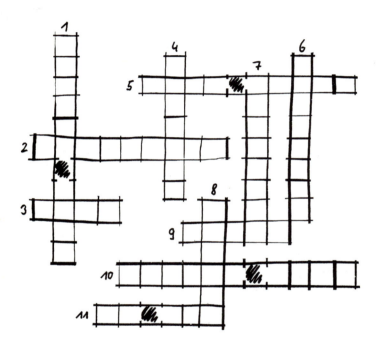

1 Doppelzimmer
2 Telefon
3 buchen
4 Balkon
5 Halbpension
6 Badezimmer
7 Prospekt
8 Toilette
9 Hotel
10 Einzelzimmer
11 Fernseher

## 20  Einen Flug buchen

### Telefon call

woman: Heathrow Airport, information desk, good morning. Can I help you?

Ms. Burns: Good morning. This is Ms. Burns speaking. I'd like to book a flight to Brazil for Wednesday.

woman: I'm sorry, Ms. Burns, but this flight is fully booked.

Ms. Burns: What about Thursday, then?

woman: Yes, there is a flight on Thursday. Shall I book a seat for you on Thursday?

Ms. Burns: Yes, please. Can I also confirm the return flight for the 30th?

woman: Yes, certainly. You can fly with Lufthansa.

Ms. Burns: When do I have to be at the airport for my flight to Brazil?

woman: Just be here an hour before the flight. Go to the check-in desk and there you get your boarding pass and your airline ticket.

Ms. Burns: Which gate is it?

woman: It's gate number ten.

Ms. Burns: I'd like a seat near the toilet but also at a window.

woman: Okay. You can take seat number 64.

Ms. Burns: But I don't want to sit over the wings.

woman: Let's see. Then you can have seat number 33.

Ms. Burns: And I don't want to sit near any children.

woman: Just a moment. That should be no problem. And where would you like us to install the cockpit?

## Telefongespräch

| | |
|---|---|
| Frau: | Flughafen Heathrow, Information, guten Morgen. Kann ich Ihnen helfen? |
| Ms. Burns: | Guten Morgen. Hier spricht Ms. Burns. Ich würde gerne einen Flug nach Brasilien für Mittwoch buchen. |
| Frau: | Es tut mir leid Ms. Burns, aber dieser Flug ist ausgebucht. |
| Ms. Burns: | Wie steht es mit Donnerstag? |
| Frau: | Ja, es gibt einen Flug am Donnerstag. Soll ich Ihnen einen Platz für Donnerstag reservieren? |
| Ms. Burns: | Ja, bitte. Kann ich auch gleich den Rückflug für den 30. bestätigt bekommen? |
| Frau: | Ja, natürlich. Sie können mit der Lufthansa fliegen. |

| | |
|---|---|
| Ms. Burns: | Wann muss ich am Flughafen sein, wenn ich nach Brasilien fliege? |
| Frau: | Seien Sie eine Stunde vor dem Start hier. Gehen Sie zum Abfertigungsschalter und dort werden Sie Ihre Bordkarte und Ihren Flugschein bekommen. |
| Ms. Burns: | Welcher Flugsteig wird es sein? |
| Frau: | Flugsteig Nummer zehn. |
| Ms. Burns: | Ich hätte gerne einen Sitzplatz in der Nähe der Toiletten, aber auch am Fenster. |
| Frau: | Gut. Sie können den Platz Nummer 64 bekommen. |
| Ms. Burns: | Aber ich möchte nicht in der Nähe der Tragflächen sitzen. |
| Frau: | Lassen Sie mich überlegen. Dann können Sie Platz Nummer 33 nehmen. |
| Ms. Burns: | Und ich möchte nicht in der Nähe von Kindern sitzen. |
| Frau: | Einen Augenblick. Ja, das können wir einrichten. Und wo sollen wir für Sie das Cockpit anbringen? |

## A Bringen Sie bitte die durcheinander geratenen Sätze in die richtige Reihenfolge.

1. I/book/flight/want/a/to.

2. is/Sunday/flight/there/on/a?

_____

3. you/confirm/return/can/the/also/flight?

_____

4. fly/can/you/with/Lufthansa.

_____

5. your/at/check-in desk/get/pass/boarding/the/you.

_____

6. is/number/it/gate/eight.

_____


**B Übersetzen Sie bitte die folgenden Begriffe.**

1. Ausgang

_____

2. Rückflug

_____

3. Flugschein

_____

4. Tragflächen

_____

## 21 Privates

### Telefon call

The phone rings. Sally is at home and picks up the receiver.

| | |
|---|---|
| Sally: | Hello, this is Sally Ingram speaking. |
| Grandfather: | Hello Sally, this is your Grandpa John speaking from Leicester. |
| Sally: | Oh, hello Grandpa, how are you? |
| Grandfather: | I'm fine, what about you? |
| Sally: | Thank you, I'm fine, too, but I have a lot of work to do this week. |
| Grandfather: | I see. What about the children? |
| Sally: | The children are at school at the moment. They are doing well. Toby was ill last week but now he's feeling much better. What about Grandma? |
| Grandfather: | She sits in the garden all the time. She is a little unhappy with the telephone I bought last week. |
| Sally: | You bought a new telephone? |
| Grandfather: | Yes, a green one with buttons on it instead of a dial. |
| Sally: | Grandma is unhappy with the buttons? |
| Grandfather: | No, the telephone cord is too long. She is always stumbling over the cord. |
| Sally: | What about shortening the cord? |
| Grandfather: | That's the reason why I phoned. |
| Sally: | But what can I do to help? |
| Grandfather: | Just pull it back a little from your end, will you? |

**cord    Kabel, Schnur**

# Telefongespräch

Das Telefon klingelt. Sally ist zu Hause und nimmt den Hörer ab.

Sally: Hallo, hier spricht Sally Ingram.
Großvater: Hallo Sally, hier ist Opa John aus Leicester.
Sally: Oh, hallo Opa, wie geht's?
Großvater: Mir geht's gut, und dir?
Sally: Mir geht's auch gut. Aber ich muss viel arbeiten.
Großvater: Ich verstehe. Wie geht es den Kindern?
Sally: Die Kinder sind gerade in der Schule. Toby war letzte Woche krank, aber nun geht es ihm schon viel besser. Wie geht es Oma?
Großvater: Sie sitzt die ganze Zeit im Garten. Sie ist etwas unzufrieden mit dem Telefon, das ich letzte Woche gekauft habe.
Sally: Du hast ein neues Telefon gekauft?
Großvater: Ja, ein grünes mit Knöpfen anstelle einer Wählscheibe.
Sally: Oma ist unzufrieden mit diesen Knöpfen?
Großvater: Nein, die Telefonschnur ist zu lang. Sie stolpert immer über die Schnur.
Sally: Warum kürzt man die Schnur nicht?
Großvater: Das ist der Grund, warum ich dich anrufe.
Sally: Aber was kann ich zu deiner Unterstützung tun?
Großvater: Zieh sie einfach ein bisschen von deinem Ende aus zurück, kannst du das?

## A  Übersetzen Sie diesen Dialog bitte ins Englische.

1. Cindy: Hallo, hier spricht Cindy Height.
2. Richard: Hallo Cindy, hier spricht Richard.
3. Cindy: Hallo Richard, wie geht es dir?
4. Richard: Mir geht es gut, und dir?
5. Cindy: Mir geht es auch gut.
6. Richard: Was macht Charlotte?
7. Cindy: Sie ist nicht zu Hause.
8. Richard: Das war der Grund meines Anrufes.

1. Cindy: _____
2. Richard: _____
3. Cindy: _____
4. Richard: _____
5. Cindy: _____
6. Richard: _____
7. Cindy: _____
8. Richard: _____

## B  Übersetzen Sie bitte ins Englische.

1. Telefonhörer _____
2. Wählscheibe _____
3. Wähltasten _____

Lösungen Seite 123

# 22 Liebe

**Letter**

April 22, 1998

My dearest Bridget,

I have been sitting beside my telephone since we first met on Friday. I cannot call you on the phone, because you forgot to give me your number. Why didn't you ring me up? I am waiting full of longing.
I fell in love with you at first sight and since then my life has totally changed. I remember you sitting there in that street café with this beautiful dress on. The wind was playing in your long dark hair and your smile made me want to spend the rest of my life with you. Oh, Bridget! Later, when I brought you home, I felt like I was standing on air. Your voice is so sweet, I wished I could listen to it the whole night through. Or to say it in Shakespeare's words: "How silver sweet sound lovers' tongues by night, like softest music to attending ears." I long for your presence and cannot stop thinking of you. When will we meet again? You said you have to visit your old sick grandma on Monday, to play tennis on Tuesday, to go to the hairdresser on Wednesday and to clean your flat on Thursday. Next weekend you are going on a long journey, you said.
When can we meet, then? I can get off any time you like. When does it suit you best? I'll be absolutely guided by you. Just call me and I'll be standing at your door. Will you?

Forever yours, Charlie

# Brief

22. April 1998

Liebste Bridget,

seit wir uns am Freitag das erste Mal gesehen haben, sitze ich neben meinem Telefon. Ich kann dich nicht anrufen, denn du hast vergessen, mir deine Telefonnummer zu geben. Warum hast du mich nicht angerufen? Ich warte sehnsüchtig. Ich habe mich auf den ersten Blick in dich verliebt und seitdem hat sich mein Leben komplett verändert. Ich erinnere mich daran, wie du in dem Straßencafé gesessen hast mit diesem schönen Kleid an. Der Wind spielte in deinem langen dunklen Haar und dein Lächeln erweckte in mir den Wunsch, den Rest meines Lebens mit dir zu verbringen. Oh Bridget! Später, als ich dich nach Hause brachte, glaubte ich zu schweben. Deine Stimme ist so süß, ich wünschte, ich könnte sie die ganze Nacht hören. Oder, um es mit Shakespeare auszudrücken: „Wie silbern-süß klingen die Zungen Liebender bei Nacht, wie leiseste Musik für aufmerksame Ohren!" Ich sehne mich nach deiner Gegenwart und kann nicht aufhören, an dich zu denken. Wann werden wir uns wieder treffen? Du sagtest, du musst am Montag deine alte kranke Großmutter besuchen, am Dienstag Tennis spielen, am Mittwoch zum Friseur und am Donnerstag deine Wohnung sauber machen. Du sagtest, nächstes Wochenende würdest du eine lange Reise antreten. Wann können wir uns denn treffen? Ich kann mich freimachen, wann immer es dir passt. Wann passt es dir am besten? Ich richte mich ganz nach dir. Ruf mich einfach an und ich stehe vor deiner Tür. Tust du das?

Dein für immer, Charlie

**A Kreuzen Sie bitte die Formulierungen an, die man am ehesten in einem Liebesbrief finden wird.**

1.
- [ ] I had a fight with a knight.
- [ ] I fell in the hole, 'cause there was no light.
- [ ] I fell in love at first sight.

2.
- [ ] The wind was playing in your hair.
- [ ] The bricks were laid with care.
- [ ] The wind confused the mare.

3.
- [ ] I feel that he doesn't even care.
- [ ] I melt in unconditioned air.
- [ ] I felt like I was standing on air.

4.
- [ ] I need another sheet.
- [ ] Your voice is so sweet.
- [ ] I have no book to read.

5.
- [ ] That doesn't make any sense.
- [ ] I'm in the wrong residence.
- [ ] I long for your presence.

# 23 Geburtstag

**Letter**

March 23, 1998

Dear Ian,

Knowing that you'll be thirty this year, I've taken great pains not to be late this time.
Well, then, here are my best wishes for a happy birthday and many happy returns of the day. In particular, I wish you happiness, good health, and success in your professional life throughout the next ten years. Being thirty myself, I know that things get more difficult in life. Your hair will get thinner, your gut will get fatter and you will discover the first wrinkles in your face. Getting up early will be a problem after a party.
But there are worse things than losing your youthfulness (although I can't think of an example at present).
I hope your birthday party will be a success; real friends are hard to find when you get older, I tell you. So, take care of yourself and once again: many happy returns!
I hope it won't be long before we see each other again.

Yours,
Brian

| | |
|---:|:---|
| great pains | große Mühe |
| professional life | Berufsleben |
| belly | Bauch |
| wrinkles | Falten |
| youthfulness | Jugendlichkeit |
| at present | jetzt |

# Brief

23. März 1998

Lieber Ian,

da ich weiß, dass du dieses Jahr dreißig wirst, habe ich mir große Mühe gegeben, dieses Mal rechtzeitig zu sein. Nun denn, hier sind meine besten Wünsche zum Geburtstag, dem hoffentlich noch viele folgen. Im Einzelnen wünsche ich dir Zufriedenheit, Gesundheit und Erfolg für deinen beruflichen Werdegang in den nächsten zehn Jahren.
Da ich selbst dreißig bin, weiß ich, dass es im Leben schwieriger wird. Dein Haar wird dünner, dein Bauch wird dicker und du wirst die ersten Falten in deinem Gesicht entdecken. Frühes Aufstehen nach einer Party wird zum Problem.
Aber es gibt Schlimmeres, als die Jugendlichkeit zu verlieren (mir will nur gerade nicht ein einziges Beispiel einfallen).
Ich hoffe, deine Geburtstagsparty wird ein voller Erfolg. Echte Freunde sind schwer zu finden, wenn man älter wird, das kannst du mir glauben.
Also, pass auf dich auf und noch einmal: Herzlichen Glückwunsch!
Ich hoffe, es wird nicht zu lange dauern, bis wir uns mal wiedersehen.

Viele Grüße
dein Brian

**A  Kreuzen Sie bitte die richtigen Antworten an. Es ist jeweils mehr als eine Antwort richtig!**

1. What do you say if you want to congratulate a friend on his birthday?
- ☐ Congratulations!
- ☐ Many happy returns of the day!
- ☐ What a pity!
- ☐ My best wishes for a happy birthday!
- ☐ Happy Easter!

2. What are your wishes for a friend on her or his birthday?
- ☐ wrinkles
- ☐ health
- ☐ thin hair
- ☐ happiness
- ☐ a thick belly

**B  Schreiben Sie bitte eine kleine Grußkarte an eine Freundin/einen Freund, in der Sie ihr/ihm gratulieren und zusätzlich einige nette Dinge wünschen.**

# 24 Weihnachten

**Card**

December 18, 1998

My dear Sandra,

Carol has gone out Christmas shopping and I am using this opportunity to write all my Christmas cards.
I want to wish you a Merry Christmas and a Happy New Year. May all your wishes come true on Christmas Eve. On Christmas Day we will be meeting our friends in the neighbourhood and we'll eat Christmas goose together; on Boxing Day Carol's parents will arrive and stay for two days. I hope dearest darling mother-in-law will not give me another bottle of aftershave this Christmas. Thanks to her generosity I am already the proud owner of an enormous aftershave collection. She ignores the fact that I've had a full beard since I was twenty-two. Maybe I should take it as a little hint that she doesn't like my outward appearance. Have a nice holiday and look after yourself.

                                              Yours,
                                              Thomas

| | |
|---:|:---|
| **opportunity** | **Gelegenheit** |
| **neighbourhood** | **Nachbarschaft** |
| **mother-in-law** | **Schwiegermutter** |
| **generosity** | **Großzügigkeit** |
| **collection** | **Sammlung** |
| **to ignore** | **ignorieren** |
| **outward appearance** | **Aussehen** |
| **hint** | **Hinweis** |

**Karte**

18. Dezember 1998

Liebe Sandra,

Carol macht Weihnachtseinkäufe und ich nutze diese Gelegenheit, um Weihnachtskarten zu schreiben.
Ich möchte dir fröhliche Weihnachten wünschen und einen guten Rutsch ins neue Jahr. Mögen alle deine Wünsche am Heiligen Abend in Erfüllung gehen.
Am ersten Weihnachtstag werden wir uns mit Freunden aus der Nachbarschaft treffen und eine Weihnachtsgans essen und am zweiten Weihnachtstag kommen Carols Eltern und bleiben für zwei Tage hier.
Ich hoffe, meine liebe Schwiegermutter wird mir zu Weihnachten nicht noch ein Aftershave schenken. Dank ihrer Großzügigkeit bin ich der stolze Besitzer einer beachtlichen Aftershave–Sammlung. Sie ignoriert die Tatsache, dass ich seit meinem 22. Lebensjahr einen Vollbart trage. Vielleicht soll ich das als kleinen Hinweis verstehen, dass ihr mein Aussehen nicht gefällt.

Schöne Ferien und bleibe gesund.

Viele Grüße,
Thomas

**A  Füllen Sie bitte den Lückentext mit den unten angegebenen Wörtern aus.**

_____Tom,

I wish you a _____ Christmas and a _____.
May all your _____ come true on Christmas _____.
I've already done the Christmas _____ and now I
have to prepare the meal. We're having a _____ for
Christmas dinner. On Christmas _____ we'll be staying
at home and on _____ Day we're visiting the
neighbours.

Have a nice _____ and keep well.
_____, Tim

**goose, Yours, Merry, Day, wishes, Happy New Year, holiday, Boxing, Dear, shopping**

**B  Eine Scherzfrage!**

Who's Santa Claus's wife?

# 25  Große Feste

## Formal invitation

Lady Harriett Sunderland
at Home

Sunday June 26th at 8.00 pm

Lady Harriett Sunderland requests the pleasure of your company at the yearly dinner and dance at Blackforest House.
We would be very pleased if you and your wife could arrange to come to this event.
We hope that Sir James will be willing to play the piano that evening.
Please be sure to wear suitable clothes (no trainers) for this formal occasion and please confirm your acceptance of this invitation in writing.

Yours sincerely,
Lady Harriett Sunderland

| | |
|---:|:---|
| to request | **erbitten** |
| pleasure | **Vergnügen** |
| event | **Ereignis** |
| company | **Gesellschaft** |
| wife | **Gattin** |
| suitable | **passend** |
| trainers | **Sportbekleidung** |
| ceremonial | **feierlich** |
| occasion | **Gelegenheit** |
| invitation | **Einladung** |
| sincerely | **hochachtungsvoll** |

## Formelle Einladung

Lady Harriett Sunderland
im Hause

Sonntag, den 26. Juni um 20.00 Uhr


Lady Harriett Sunderland erbittet das Vergnügen Ihrer Anwesenheit bei der jährlichen Abendgesellschaft in Blackforest House.
Wir wären sehr erfreut, wenn Sie und Ihre Gattin es einrichten könnten, zu diesem Ereignis zu erscheinen.
Wir haben große Hoffnung, dass Sir James einwilligt, an diesem Abend das Piano zu spielen.
Tragen Sie bitte angemessene Kleidung (keine Sportbekleidung) zu diesem feierlichen Anlass und bestätigen Sie diese Einladung bitte schriftlich.

Hochachtungsvoll,
Lady Harriett Sunderland

# 26 Kleine Feiern

## Informal invitation

Dear Robert and Joan,

I wonder if you would be free on 26th June.
We are going to have a garden party, because we have new neighbours, the Wisemans. They are very nice people and I'm sure you'll like them. We would be very happy if you could come along that evening.
We will have a barbecue and Lenny will be the barman. Some of his cocktails can blow your mind, so, Robert, be careful this time!
Harry and his band will also be here and they have promised to play for us. You will remember that Harry is always the life and soul of successful parties. Please let me know if you can join our party.

Yours,
David

| | |
|---:|---|
| to wonder | sich fragen |
| barbecue | Grillen |
| to blow one's mind | umhauen |
| life and soul | Herz und Seele |

## Informelle Einladung

Lieber Robert und liebe Joan,

ich frage mich, ob ihr am 26. Juni wohl Zeit habt.
Wir werden eine Gartenparty veranstalten, weil wir neue Nachbarn haben, die Wisemans. Es sind sehr nette Leute und ich bin sicher, dass ihr sie mögt. Wir würden uns sehr freuen, wenn ihr an diesem Abend kommen könntet.
Wir werden grillen und Lenny wird der Barkeeper sein. Einige seiner Cocktails können dich umhauen, Robert, sei dieses Mal vorsichtig!
Harry und seine Band werden auch kommen und sie haben versprochen, für uns zu spielen. Du erinnerst dich sicher, dass Harry immer das Herz und die Seele gelungener Parties ist.
Sagt uns bitte Bescheid, ob ihr kommt.

Viele Grüße,
David

**A  Ordnen Sie bitte die nachfolgenden Satzteile den Bereichen „formell" oder „ungezwungen" zu.**

1. garden party
2. I request the pleasure of your company
3. confirm this invitation in writing
4. yours sincerely
5. we would be very happy

6. I wonder if you will be free
7. dinner party
8. wear suitable clothes
9. let me know if you can come to the party
10. yours,
11. we would be very pleased
12. successful party
13. ceremonial occasion
14. Dear Robert and Joan,

|     | formell | ungezwungen |
|-----|---------|-------------|
| 1.  | ☐       | ☐           |
| 2.  | ☐       | ☐           |
| 3.  | ☐       | ☐           |
| 4.  | ☐       | ☐           |
| 5.  | ☐       | ☐           |
| 6.  | ☐       | ☐           |
| 7.  | ☐       | ☐           |
| 8.  | ☐       | ☐           |
| 9.  | ☐       | ☐           |
| 10. | ☐       | ☐           |
| 11. | ☐       | ☐           |
| 12. | ☐       | ☐           |
| 13. | ☐       | ☐           |
| 14. | ☐       | ☐           |

Lösungen Seite 125

*Kleine Feiern*

## 27 Unvorhersehbare Umstände

**Formal refusal**

August 20, 1998

Dear Lady Sunderland,

May I offer you our warmest thanks for your invitation. Robert and Joan Grant greatly regret that they are unable to accept your kind invitation for the 26th owing to unforeseen circumstances.

It has always been a great pleasure for us to be your guests at Blackforest House. Sir James is a gifted piano player and you can imagine how unhappy we are that we shall be unable to listen to his lovely melodies this year.

I hope your four delightful little dogs are bouncing around fit and well. Robert was very fond of them and could not stop tickling them under the chin.

Please convey our apologies to Lord Sunderland and tell him that it is a great disappointment to us. We shall really miss seeing you.

Yours sincerely,
Joan Grant

| | |
|---:|:---|
| **unforeseen circumstances** | unvorhersehbare Umstände |
| **gifted** | begnadet |
| **delightful** | entzückend |
| **to bounce** | herumspringen |
| **to be fond of s.th.** | von etwas angetan sein |
| **to tickle** | kraulen |
| **chin** | Kinn |
| **to convey** | übermitteln |

# Formelle Absage

20. August 1998

Sehr geehrte Lady Sunderland,

ich möchte mich recht herzlich für Ihre Einladung bedanken.
Robert und Joan Grant müssen sich leider entschuldigen und können Ihre Einladung für den 26. Juni aufgrund unvorhersehbarer Umstände nicht annehmen.
Es war uns jedesmal ein großes Vergnügen, Gast in Blackforest House zu sein. Sir James ist ein begnadeter Klavierspieler und Sie können sich vorstellen, wie unglücklich wir darüber sind, dieses Jahr nicht seinen reizenden Melodien lauschen zu dürfen.
Ich hoffe, Ihre vier entzückenden kleinen Hunde springen munter umher. Robert war sehr von ihnen angetan und konnte gar nicht aufhören, sie unter dem Kinn zu kraulen. Entschuldigen Sie uns bitte auch bei Lord Sunderland und sagen Sie ihm, dass es uns wirklich sehr leid tut. Wir finden es wirklich schade, dass wir Sie nicht sehen werden.

Hochachtungsvoll,
Joan Grant

**Sie wollen sich für eine sehr formelle Einladung bedanken.**

1. Sie schreiben:
□ Thank you for your nice invitation.
□ Oh God, I couldn't believe my eyes. Thank you, thank you, thank you.
□ May I offer you our warmest thanks for your invitation.
□ Great! Best news for the last two weeks.

2. Sie müssen aber leider absagen. Sie schreiben:
□ No, sorry. We won't come.
□ We are unable to accept your kind invitation.
□ Bother it! I can't come.
□ I'm sorry, but I have got some urgent things to do.

3. Sie möchten Ihr Bedauern für die Absage ausdrücken. Sie schreiben:
□ I'm sorry, but I can't see you.
□ We will be somewhere else. We cannot see you.
□ We shall really miss seeing you.
□ I really shall miss your good champagne.

4. Außerdem möchten Sie auch dem Gatten/der Gattin Ihr Bedauern ausdrücken. Sie schreiben:
□ Tell him/her that it is a great disappointment for us.
□ Tell him/her we shall be somewhere else.
□ Tell him/her I'm sorry.
□ Tell him/her that he/she can eat our dinner.

# 28 Vielen Dank

**To accept an invitation, informal**

Dear David,

Many thanks for the invitation to your party. We'd love to come and we are really looking forward to it.
Lady Sunderland's dinner party will take place the same evening, but Joan and I have decided to cancel it. I don't like those snobbish braggarts talking about playing golf all the time.
Lady Sunderland is a battleaxe and I'm thankful that this year I won't have to tickle her four smelly terriers under the chin for hours. And there was this old twit, Sir James, who played the same waltz again and again. Terrible.
Harry and his band are excellent players and I can hardly wait to hear them. No cocktails for me this time, I can assure you. Lenny's cocktails are very dangerous. I couldn't remember how I got into my bed that night.

See you on Sunday,
Robert

| | |
|---:|:---|
| braggart | Angeber |
| battleaxe | Schreckschraube |
| smelly | stinkig |
| twit | Spinner |
| waltz | Walzer |
| terrible | schrecklich |
| to assure | versichern |

## Eine Einladung annehmen, ungezwungen

Lieber David,

vielen Dank für die Einladung zu eurer Party. Wir kommen sehr gerne und können es kaum erwarten.
Lady Sunderlands Abendgesellschaft findet am selben Abend statt, aber Joan und ich haben uns entschlossen, ihr abzusagen.
Ich mag diese versnobten Angeber nicht, die die ganze Zeit über Golf reden. Lady Sunderland ist eine Schreckschraube und ich bin dankbar dafür, dass ich in diesem Jahr nicht stundenlang ihre stinkigen Terrier unter dem Kinn kraulen muss.
Und dann war da noch dieser alte Trottel, Sir James, der den gleichen Walzer immer und immer wieder spielte. Schrecklich.
Harry und seine Band sind wirklich exzellente Spieler und ich kann diesen Abend kaum erwarten. Keine Cocktails für mich dieses Mal, das verspreche ich dir. Lennys Cocktails sind tückisch. Ich konnte mich nicht erinnern, wie ich in dieser Nacht in mein Bett gekommen bin.

Wir sehen uns Sonntag,
Robert

## A  Bringen Sie bitte die Satzstücke in die richtige Reihenfolge.

1. forward/are/We/looking/really/it/to.

   _____

2. on/you/See/Sunday.

   _____

3. thanks/invitation/your/many/for.

   _____

4. David/Dear,

   _____

5. hardly/can/I/for/evening/wait/this.

   _____

6. would/come/to/We/love.

   _____


## B  Bringen Sie bitte die Sätze aus Aufgabe A in die richtige Reihenfolge, sodass ein Dankschreiben für eine Einladung entsteht.

1. ☐   2. ☐   3. ☐

4. ☐   5. ☐   6. ☐

Lösungen Seite 126

# 29  Ferien

## A greeting card

Hello Sarah,

I'm now on my trip through the most famous national parks in the USA. The weather is fine and Ellen and I are very impressed by the landscape. There are nice camping sites around and we are having a really good time.
We mostly roam through the forests looking for bears or go fishing. There are huge old trees in some areas. That reminds me of a funny event last Sunday.
We were on a guided trip with some other tourists in the national park. One nice old lady who was with us stood under a huge tree, saying: "Oh, wonderful old elm tree if you could only speak, what would you say to me?" Ellen replied: "It would probably say: 'Pardon me, lady, but I'm an oak.' "
We really couldn't stop laughing.

That's all for now,
see you,

       Betty

| | |
|---:|:---|
| to impress | beeindrucken |
| landscape | Landschaft |
| camping site | Campingplatz |
| to roam | umherwandern |
| guided | geführt |
| huge | riesig |
| elm | Ulme |
| to reply | erwidern |
| oak | Eiche |

**Eine Grußkarte**

Hallo Sarah,

ich mache gerade meine Reise durch die berühmten Nationalparks in den USA. Das Wetter ist gut und Ellen und ich sind von der Landschaft sehr beeindruckt. Es gibt hier schöne Campingplätze und wir verbringen eine wirklich schöne Zeit.
Meistens streunen wir durch die Wälder, suchen nach Bären oder gehen angeln. Es gibt in einigen Regionen sehr alte und riesige Bäume. Das erinnert mich an einen lustigen Zwischenfall am letzten Sonntag.
Wir machten eine Wanderung mit Führung und einigen anderen Touristen. Eine nette alte Dame, die dabei war, stand unter einem riesigen Baum und sagte: „Oh, wundervolle alte Ulme, wenn du nur sprechen könntest, was würdest du wohl zu mir sagen?"
Ellen antwortete ihr: „Sie würde wahrscheinlich sagen: ‚Entschuldigen Sie bitte, aber ich bin eine Eiche.'"
Wir konnten uns vor Lachen kaum halten.

Das ist alles für heute, bis bald,
Betty

# Another greeting card

Dear Mom and Dad,

here I am with Aunt Ulla and Uncle Rolf spending my holiday in Munich.
Munich is a very big and beautiful city, but I don't have much time to enjoy it, because Uncle Rolf uses every free minute to go mountain climbing. I always have to accompany him and climbing up mountains is very hard and I have to use all my strength.
Last Friday I thought I couldn't make it. I was sweating like anything and my legs were hurting. When we reached the top of the hill, Uncle Rolf was amazed by the view and said: "Look at that little village over there and that beautiful river flowing right through the middle. Can you see those tiny cows?"
I saw it all, but at the same time I was wondering why the hell we always have to climb up these stupid mountains when he thinks that it is much lovelier below in the valley?

Yours ever, Patsy

| | |
|---:|:---|
| to enjoy something | etwas genießen |
| to accompany | begleiten |
| strength | Kraft |
| to hurt | schmerzen |
| to reach | erreichen |
| to be amazed | begeistert sein |
| village | Dorf |
| to flow | fließen |
| tiny | winzig |
| stupid | dumm |
| below | unten |
| valley | Tal |

## Noch eine Urlaubskarte

Liebe Mama und lieber Papa,

hier bin ich also bei Tante Ulla und Onkel Rolf und verbringe meine Ferien in München.
München ist eine sehr schöne und große Stadt, aber ich kann nicht viel Zeit in der Stadt verbringen, weil Onkel Rolf jede freie Minute zum Bergsteigen nutzt. Ich muss ihn immer begleiten.
Bergsteigen ist sehr anstrengend und ich muss meine ganze Kraft dafür aufbringen. Letzten Freitag dachte ich, ich würde es nicht schaffen. Ich schwitzte wie ein Tier und meine Beine taten weh. Als wir auf dem Gipfel ankamen, war Onkel Rolf von der Aussicht begeistert. Er sagte: „Sieh dir dieses niedliche kleine Dorf dort drüben an und dieser hübsche Fluss in der Mitte. Kannst du diese winzigen Kühe sehen?"
Ich konnte das alles sehen, aber gleichzeitig fragte ich mich, warum zur Hölle wir immer diese dummen Berge hinaufsteigen müssen, wenn er meint, dass es unten im Tal viel zauberhafter ist.

Viele Grüße,
Patsy

**A  Füllen Sie bitte die Lücken im Text aus, indem Sie die nachstehenden deutschen Wörter übersetzen.**

_____ Sally,

I'm on my _____ (Reise) through Canada.

The _____ (Wetter) is _____ (gut) and I'm having

a jolly good _____ (Zeit).

Sometimes I go _____ (bergsteigen) and

sometimes I go _____ (angeln). There are many

_____ (Wälder) in Canada and some of the

_____ (Bäume) are very _____ (alt).

The _____ (Landschaft) is absolutely _____

(schön) and there are wonderful _____

(Campingplätze).

_____ (Viele Grüße,) Lucy

**B  Schreiben Sie bitte eine Urlaubskarte, in der Sie sagen, dass ...**
1. Sie sich auf einer Reise in Irland befinden
2. das Wetter schön ist
3. die Landschaft zauberhaft ist
4. es keine Berge oder Wälder gibt
5. Dublin eine schöne Stadt ist
6. Sie eine schöne Zeit verbringen

*Korrespondenz*

Lösungen Seite 127

# Lösungen

## 1   Hotel

1. I have room number 208.
2. There is a problem with the shower.
3. Can you help me?
4. I'll try my very best.
5. Where is the telephone?
6. Where is the reception desk?
7. Will you be so kind?
8. There is another little problem.
9. Just leave it to me.
10. I tell you, I've seen a mouse!

## 2   Frühstück im Hotel

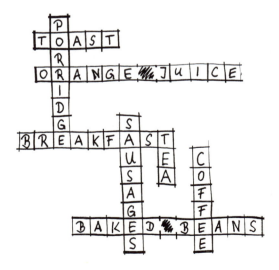

**B**

It's a teapot.

### 3  Telefonieren mit Geld

**A**

1. Have enough coins ready.
2. Dial a 1 for long distance calls.
3. Dial the area code.
4. Dial the rest of the number.
5. A computer voice will tell you how many coins you have to put in.
6. You are connected.

**B**

1. Dial a 0 for long distance calls.
2. Dial the area code.
3. A voice tells you to enter your private number.
4. You enter your home number plus a 4 digit PIN code.
5. A computer voice thanks you.
6. You are connected.

**C**

1. Die *private number* setzt sich zusammen aus der eigenen Telefonnummer plus einer vierstelligen Geheimzahl.
2. Jeder Staat hat einen eigenen *area code*. Der *area code* ist sozusagen die Vorwahl für einen bestimmten Staat.

## 4 Telefonieren ohne Geld

**A**
1. Take the receiver.
2. Dial a 0 and the rest of your number.
3. The voice will tell you to wait for an operator.
4. Voice asks you to say your name after the "beep".
5. You say your name after the "beep".
6. A computer calls the number of the people you want to talk to.
7. The computer asks the people if they want to accept the call.
8. The people say "yes".
9. You are connected.

**B**
1. I want to call collect.
2. I hope they will accept the call.
3. I'm waiting for an operator.
4. I was disconnected.

## 5 Arzt

**A**

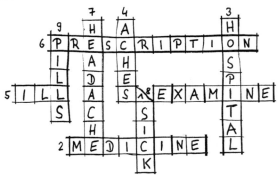

**B**

Es ist die Mutter.
In der englischen Sprache gelten die meisten Berufsbezeichnungen für beide Geschlechter. In der deutschen Sprache ist das anders. Daher haben die Deutschen zumeist eine männliche Person vor Augen, wenn nur der Beruf genannt wird.

## 6   Apotheke

**A**

1. sneezing, 2. pains, 3. headache, 4. vitamins, 5. plaster

**B**

1. You should buy a pain-reliever.
2. I'm not too well.
3. I've got stomach ache.
4. I'm sneezing all the time.
5. Take some of these vitamin pills.

**C**

1. chemist's, 2. a cure, 3. a pain reliever

## 7   Post

1. parcel; 2. counter assistant; 3. envelope;
4. address; 5. postman; 6. postcard;
7. stamps; 8. collection; 9. letter; 10. scales;
11. post office

## 8  Supermarkt

**A**

1. We need a dozen eggs.
2. Shall we have this chocolate bar?
3. Don't ask for luxury goods!
4. What about ice-cream?
5. Will you go and fetch some bananas?
6. No, it is too expensive!
7. We also need some lettuce.

**B**

1. We also need milk.
2. That is too expensive.
3. What about this one?
4. Go and look for frozen pizza.


## 9  Andenkenladen

**A**

1. Can I help you?
2. I'm looking for a souvenir.
3. This reminds me of a wonderful friend.
4. What about this one?
5. No, that's not the right thing.
6. What is it?
7. You're a swindler!

**B**

shop assistant: Good afternoon. What can I do for you?
tourist:        I'm looking for something really interesting.

shop assistant: Look at this one?
tourist: No, I already have one.
shop assistant: Now I know what you are looking for. Look at this.
tourist: What is it?
shop assistant: These are bagpipes.

## 10  Restaurant

Gutes Restaurant:
1. the fish was good
2. the service was attentive
3. the room was not crowded
4. the wine tasted good
5. one can recommend it
6. the meal was cheap

Schlechtes Restaurant:
1. the meal was expensive
2. the soup was cold
3. the fish was half raw
4. the service was snooty
5. we didn't get a table
6. the waiter was in a hurry

## 11  Nachtleben

**A**  1. opera; 2. cinema; 3. disco; 4. music bar

**B**  1. What about ...; 2. That would be real fun; 3. I really like it.


## 12 Pub

1. Tom: Hi Bill. How are you?
2. Bill: Hi Tom. I'm fine, and you?
3. Tom: Thank's I'm fine. Nice weather today, isn't it?
4. Bill: Yes, great.
5. Tom: What's yours?
6. Bill: That's nice of you. I'll take a lager.
7. Tom: What kind of book have you got in your pocket?
8. Bill: It's a guide.
9. Tom: I would like to read it, too.
10. Bill: Here you are.


## 13 Getränke bestellen

1. Give me the beverage list, please.
2. I'm thirsty.
3. I would like to have something alcoholic.
4. I have a hangover.
5. I want to keep a clear head.
6. Alcohol doesn't agree with me.
7. I felt a bit tipsy.
8. I wasn't drunk.
9. I'm sorry, but we are out of mineral water.

## 14 Wetter

### A
1. It's sunny. The sun is shining.
2. It's a little cloudy. There are clouds in the sky.
3. Tomorrow there will be a thunderstorm with thunder and lightning.
4. After that it will rain.
5. In the morning it will be foggy or at least misty.
6. That's an unsettled kind of weather.

### B
What's the weather like?
1. It's sunny.
2. It's cloudy.
3. It's raining.
4. It's foggy/misty.
5. It's windy/stormy.

## 15 Nach dem Weg fragen

### A
Go straight ahead and the next street turn left. Go straight ahead to the traffic lights. Turn right until you are at a supermarket. Turn left and the very next street turn left again. You are in a park now. Cross the park and on the other side there is a bank on the right hand side. There is also a church on the left hand side. Go between them and you will see the museum on the right hand side.

**B**
You are at the theatre.

## 16 Auto

**A**
man: I want to hire a car.
woman: What about this one?
man: I don't want a Cadillac.
woman: Look at this, then.
man: I have to check the tire pressure.
woman: The tire pressure is okay.
man: I have to check the oil.
woman: The oil is also okay.
man: I don't like the colour of that car.
woman: You should hire a bicycle.

**B**
They call them tinned people.
(Sie nennen sie Menschen in Dosen.)

## 17 Fremdenverkehrsbüro

1. museum; 2. park; 3. theatre; 4. cathedral; 5. castle

## 18 Bahnhof

**A**
 1. Good morning, Sir. Can I help you?

2. What's the second class fare to Dublin?
3. Single or return?
4. Return.
5. It's seven pounds, Sir.
6. Do I have to change?
7. Yes, you will have to change.
8. How long do I have to wait for the connection?
9. About two hours.
10. That's far too long. I think I'll take the car.

**B**
1. second class fare
2. single or return
3. wait
4. connection

### 19 Hotelreservierung

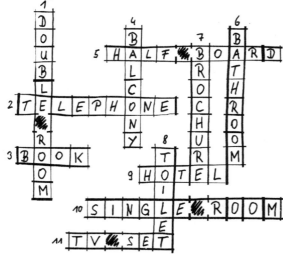

## 20 Einen Flug buchen

**A**

1. I want to book a flight.
2. Is there a flight on Sunday?
3. Can you also confirm the return flight?
4. You can fly with Lufthansa.
5. You get your boarding pass at the check-in desk.
6. It is gate number eight.

**B**

1. gate; 2. return flight; 3. boarding pass; 4. wings

## 21 Privates

**A**

1. Cindy: Hello, this is Cindy Height speaking.
2. Richard: Hello Cindy, this is Richard speaking.
3. Cindy: Hello Richard, how are you?
4. Richard: I'm fine, and how are you?
5. Cindy: I'm fine, too.
6. Richard: What about Charlotte?
7. Cindy: She's not at home.
8. Richard: That's the reason why I'm ringing you up.

**B**

1. receiver, 2. dial, 3. buttons

## 22 Liebe

1. I fell in love at first sight.
2. The wind was playing in your hair.

3. I felt like I was standing on air.
4. Your voice is so sweet.
5. I long for your presence.

## 23  Geburtstag

**A**
1.
Many happy returns of the day!
My best wishes for a happy birthday!
2.
health
happiness

**B**
Eine mögliche Version der Grußkarte:

Dear Mary,
My best wishes for a happy birthday and many happy returns of the day. I wish you health and happiness throughout the next ten years. In addition to that I wish you success in life and a wonderful birthday party.

                              Yours,
                              Harry

## 24  Weihnachten

**A**
Dear Tom,

I wish you a Merry Christmas and a Happy New Year.
May all your wishes come true on Christmas Eve.
I've already done the Christmas shopping and now I have to prepare the meal. We're having a goose for Christmas dinner. On Christmas Day we'll be staying at home and on Boxing Day we're visiting the neighbours.
Have a nice holiday and keep well,

                              Yours,
                              Tim

**B**
It's Mary Christmas.


## 25/26 Große Feste/Kleine Feiern

formell
1. I request the pleasure of your company
2. confirm this invitation in writing
3. yours sincerely
4. dinner party
5. wear suitable clothes
6. we would be very pleased
7. ceremonial occasion


ungezwungen
1. garden party
2. we would be very happy
3. I wonder if you will be free
4. let me know if you can come to the party
5. yours,
6. successful party
7. Dear Robert and Joan,

## 27 Unvorhersehbare Umstände

1. May I offer you our warmest thanks for your invitation.
2. We are unable to accept your kind invitation.
3. We shall really miss seeing you.
4. Tell him/her that it is a great disappointment for us.


## 28 Vielen Dank

### A
1. We are really looking forward to it.
2. See you on Sunday.
3. Many thanks for your invitation.
4. Dear David,
5. I can hardly wait for this evening.
6. We would love to come.

### B
1. Dear David,
2. Many thanks for your invitation.
3. We would love to come.
4. We are really looking forward to it.
5. I can hardly wait for this evening.
6. See you on Sunday.

Anmerkung: Die Sätze 4 und 5 sind natürlich auch in anderer Reihenfolge denkbar. Das bleibt Ihrem persönlichen Geschmack überlassen.

## 29 Ferien

**A**
Dear Sally,
I'm on my trip/journey through Canada. The weather is nice and I'm having a jolly good time. Sometimes I go mountain climbing and sometimes I go fishing. There are many forests in Canada and some of the trees are very old. The landscape is absolutely lovely/beautiful and there are wonderful camping sites.

Yours,
Lucy

**B**
Dear Larry,
I'm now on my trip through Ireland. The weather is nice and the landscape is lovely. There are no mountains or forests. Dublin is a very nice city. I'm having a good time here.

Yours,
Peter

Dieses Werk einschließlich aller seiner Teile ist urheberrechtlich geschützt. Jede Verwertung außerhalb des Urheberrechts ist ohne Zustimmung des Verlages unzulässig und strafbar. Das gilt insbesondere für Vervielfältigungen, Übersetzungen, Mikroverfilmungen und die Einspeicherung und Verarbeitung in elektronischen Systemen.

Der Inhalt dieses Buches ist sorgfältig recherchiert und erarbeitet worden. Dennoch können weder Autoren noch Verlag für alle Angaben im Buch eine Haftung übernehmen.

Der Text dieses Buches folgt den neuen Regeln der deutschen Rechtschreibung.

© 1998 Weltbild Verlag GmbH, Augsburg
Alle Rechte vorbehalten

Einbandgestaltung
und Titelillustration: Thomas Uhlig, Augsburg
Illustrationen: Agentur Herwig, Bornhöved (Knut Hamann)
Layout und Satz: Agentur Herwig, Bornhöved
Belichtung: Uhl + Massopust, Aalen
Druck und Bindung: Clausen & Bosse, Leck
Printed in Germany

ISBN 3-8043-4524-7